Introduction to EDUCATIONAL PSYCHOLOGY

CLEP* Test Study Guide

All rights reserved. This Study Guide, Book and Flashcards are protected under the US Copyright Law. No part of this book or study guide or flashcards may be reproduced, distributed or stored in a retrieval system, or transmitted in any form or by any means, electronic, mechanical, photocopying, recording, or otherwise, without the prior written permission of the publisher Breely Crush Publishing, LLC.

© 2022 Breely Crush Publishing, LLC

*CLEP is a registered trademark of the College Entrance Examination Board which does not endorse this book.

9710010420143

Copyright ©2003 – 2022, Breely Crush Publishing, LLC.

All rights reserved.

This Study Guide, Book and Flashcards are protected under the US Copyright Law. No part of this publication may be reproduced, distributed or stored in a retrieval system, or transmitted in any form or by any means, electronic, mechanical, photocopying, recording, or otherwise, without the prior written permission of the publisher Breely Crush Publishing, LLC.

Published by Breely Crush Publishing, LLC
10808 River Front Parkway
South Jordan, UT 84095
www.breelycrushpublishing.com

ISBN-10: 1-61433-640-7
ISBN-13: 978-1-61433-640-2

Printed and bound in the United States of America.

*CLEP is a registered trademark of the College Entrance Examination Board which does not endorse this book.

Table of Contents

Educational Aims Or Philosophies 1
    A1: Life-Long Learning 1
    A2: Moral/Character Development & Preparation For Careers 1
    A3: Preparation For Responsible Citizenship 3

Cognitive Perspective 4
    B1: Attention and Perception 4
    B2: Chunking/Encoding 5
    B3: Memory Capacity 5
    B4: Mental Imagery 5
    B5: Organization of Long-Term Memory 6
    B6: Problem Solving 7
    B7: Transfer 8
    B8: Types of Memory 9

Behavior Perspective 10
    C1: Applications of Behaviorism 10
    C2: Behavioral Modification Programs 11
    C3: Classical Conditioning 11
    C4: Cognitive Learning Theory 12
    C5: Law of Effect, Operant Conditioning, Premack Principle,
        Schedules of Reinforcement and Token Economies 13

Development 14
    D1: Adolescence 14
    D2: Cognitive Development 15
    D3: Gender Identity/Sex Roles 15
    D4: Language Acquisition 16
    D5: Mental Health 17
    D6: Moral Development 18
    D7: School Readiness 18
    D8: Social Development 19
    D9: Learning Theories 22
    D10: Memory 23
    D11: Measuring Intelligence 24
    D12: Convergent Thinking 25
    D13: Carol Gilligan and Moral Development 26

Motivation 26
    E1: Achievement Motivation – Anxiety/Stress 27
    E2: Locus of Control/Attribution Theory; Learned
        Helplessness, Intrinsic Motivation 28
    E3: Theories of Motivation 28

Individual Differences *32*
    F1: Aptitude/Achievement *32*
    F2: Creativity *32*
    F3: Cultural Influences *34*
    F4: Exceptionalities In Learning: Giftedness, Physical Handicaps,
        Behavior Disorders *35*
    F5: Intelligence *37*
    F6: Nature vs. Nurture *38*
    F7: Reading Ability *39*
Testing *39*
    G1: Assessment of Instructional Objectives; Bias in Testing;
        Classroom Assessment *39*
    G2: Descriptive Statistics; Norm and Criterion-Referenced Tests;
        Scales Score/Standard Deviation *41*
    G3: Test Construction; Test Reliability; Test Validity; Use and
        Misuse of Assessment Techniques *43*
Pedagogy *44*
    H1: Advance Organizers; Bilingual/ESL Instruction; Clarity/
        Organization *44*
    H2: Classroom Management; Cooperative Learning; Discovery
        and Reception Learning *45*
    H3: Instructional Design and Technique; Psychology of Content Areas;
        Teacher Expectation/Pygmalion
        Effect/Wait-Time *47*
Research, Design and Analysis *48*
    I1: The Scientific Method; Research Methods; Reading Charts and
        Graphs; Experiments *48*
    I2: Research Analysis and Statistics *55*
Government In Education *56*
    J1: Idea *56*
    J2: Public Law 94-142 ....*56*
Sample Test Questions *57*
Test Taking Strategies *98*
What Your Score Means *99*
Test Preparation *99*
Legal Note *100*

Introduction to Educational Psychology

 # Educational Aims or Philosophies

The general principle of education is that it should reflect the country's culture. It should aim to teach higher knowledge and skills including computer and Internet literacy. In 1.S. schools, the functions have expanded exponentially and some functions rival that of families. (e.g., childcare).

A1: LIFE-LONG LEARNING

What did we learn at schools when we were children? (a) Information (both verbal and non-verbal), (b) Skills on the intellectual plane, (c) Cognitive strategies (learning, remembering, thinking, problem-solving, etc., helping an individual to reach personal and social objectives), (d) Motor skills, and, (e) Attitudes: (changes in behavior pattern for the better). There are many stages in a man's life and whatever he learns helps him to adapt himself to the changing 'life course.' (1) Childhood (up to 12 yrs of age) (2) Adolescence (Ages 13 to17/18) (3) Young adulthood (Ages 18-29) (4) Early middle age (Ages 30-49) (5) Late middle age (Ages 50-65) and (6) Old age. (Above 65 yrs.), are the stages in one's life.

At every stage we learn. Through college completion we learn what we are taught. Afterwards we learn from everyone, from every situation, from every minute! We learn even from a child of 2 yrs! Educating oneself is a continuous process. It is a lifelong learning process.

A2: MORAL/CHARACTER DEVELOPMENT & PREPARATION FOR CAREERS

If a person's values, personality and beliefs are added up, you get the character of that person. It is seen by others in our behavior, in our actions and in our articulations. Character building and development starts the day an individual is born and continues till his death. The quality of steel is identified with its carbon-content. The quality of person is determined by his character. One should have uniform consistency in one's total integrity, unselfish approach, precise understanding, steely conviction, formidable courage, unflinching loyalty and exceptional respect to have an excellent character. Early childhood character development starts at home and then spills over to the school, college and then to the work place. Schools allot time for character-building. Moral character education is all the more necessary because "…able and educated leaders who lack character are dangerous, for they use their abilities for selfish or anti-social ends…" [Educational Policies Commission, 'Education of the gifted'] Moral Character development does not have any structured formula to follow, nor does one use a magic wand, say 'abracadabra,' and presto develop you into a morally developed person. It is an onerous building effort. Only brick by brick can it proceed. H.L. Smith in his "Program for Character Education" had described succinctly what is needed for Moral Character Development.

"… Naturally, the work in character development must be chosen and prepared according to grade and age levels. There are, however, certain patterns of influence and effort that run continuously through all public school age levels. The following are examples:

a. The general school environment and atmosphere.
b. The influence of administrators and teachers.
c. The use of the regular curriculum.
d. Orientation, guidance and adjustment efforts.
e. Appeals (either to groups or to individuals) to reason and common sense.
f. Student participation in class, school, or school and community affairs.
g. Habit-forming experiences in class, in the school building, or on the playground.
h. Planning and incidental emphasis on character traits, ideals and moral principles…"

PREPARATION FOR CAREERS:

Both boys and girls worry about which vocation they have to choose, which will turn out to be most suitable for their self-perceived skills and knowledge. This sort of worry builds up when they reach the end of their academic life after which they have no choice but to choose their vocation. Adolescence and vocational choice go hand in hand! Young people have scant knowledge about the working world – business, industrial and commercial. Normally they are confused and thus the schools have a responsibility to help students to see their strengths and weaknesses are highlighted so that they can really know which vocation will suit them. A summary of 'Job-Descriptions' and 'Job-Specifications' should be made available to the class. Information on occupations should be made available to students in the classroom. The idea here is for the school to provide relevant information so that students get knowledge on the working world outside of which they are not a part so far: (a) Vocational reading-material can be supplied by the school. (b) Actual people of vocations can be called to share their knowledge. (c) Students can be taken to various units for first-hand knowledge on different vocations. (d) Videos, CD's, even movie clips about various vocations can be viewed, which show how skills and knowledge are translated into action. What is important is that the student should be made to realize his self-concepts and know exactly where his strength lies.

A3: *PREPARATION FOR RESPONSIBLE CITIZENSHIP*

Citizenship has real meaning only in a Democracy. It has no meaning in a totalitarian state, nor a dictatorship. Citizenship may be through birth or by domicile. Citizenship, according to the dictionary, is the legal right of belonging to a particular country. The offers its citizens (a) Individualism (b) Liberty (c) Equality (d) A society, which is wide open where freedom of speech and action thrives, and (e) Limitations imposed on Governance so that no corrupt practices flourish. A teacher should prepare a child to be a responsible citizen. A child should know the difference between Democracy and Totalitarianism as well as Dictatorship in order to appreciate citizenship. He should be taught about the values of individualism, liberty and equality. The openness of the society in which he lives should be highlighted. He should be taught about his duties and responsibilities. He should be taught about his responsibility to uphold the cultural values of his country. He should be told about his right of freedom of speech and his duty to see that this freedom does not encroach on others.

SOCIALIZATION: This is a continuous process in a human being. The best definition of socialization was given by C.Kluckhohn and H.A. Murray (eds.) – "Personality in Nature, Society, and Culture."

"…Beginning in the nursery, the process of socialization continues throughout life. Among other things, what must be learned is: the power to inhibit, or to moderate, the expression of unacceptable needs; the ability to transfer cathexis from a prohibited goal-object to an acceptable substitute; the habitual and automatic use of a large number of approved action patterns (methods, manners, and emotional attitudes); and the ability to adapt to schedules (to do things at the proper time, keep appointments, etc.). It is assumed that, having acquired these abilities, the average person will be capable of establishing satisfactory interpersonal relations within the legal and conventional framework of society. When the child begins to behave in a predictable, expectable manner it is well on the road to being socialized…"

Human beings are social animals. They are gregarious. We are born with latent potential to develop a "self" but it has to be tinkered with and tailored to suit the society we live in. In a nutshell, social-interaction molds a child's "self." C.H. Cooley propounded the "looking-glass self" according to which a child's "Self" develops as we internalize other's reaction to us. According to G.H. Mead, 'taking the role of others' is essential for the development of "Self." We will see in a later Module how a child develops the ability to reason. In addition to "id," "ego" and "super-ego," a child's personality and "Self" develops on account of interaction of social factors like, 'social classes,' 'gender,' 'religion,' 'education,' etc. How we feel, what sort of emotions we churn out, and, how our emotions are expressed are definitely influenced by socialization.

Gender plays an important in socialization. Gender socialization happens when males and females are aware of the different roles they are expected to play. Agents of socialization are: (1) family, (2) religion, (3) daycare, (4) school, (5) peer groups, and (6) the workplace. When we learn new norms, value-systems, attitudes and behaviors-patterns, we are on the road to "Re-socialization."

Socialization happens through the "Life course," more of which we will see in a later Module. It is a continuous process and does not stop when schooling or adolescences ends.

 Cognitive Perspective

B1: ATTENTION AND PERCEPTION

What is attention? We can do no better than quote Morgan, J.B and Gilliland A.R, ("An Introduction to Psychology"), whose definition covers it amply. "…Attention is being keenly alive to some specific factor in our environment. It is a preparatory adjustment response…" of the very many classifications of attention, the one given by J.S. Ross (Ground Work of Educational Psychology) is acceptable.

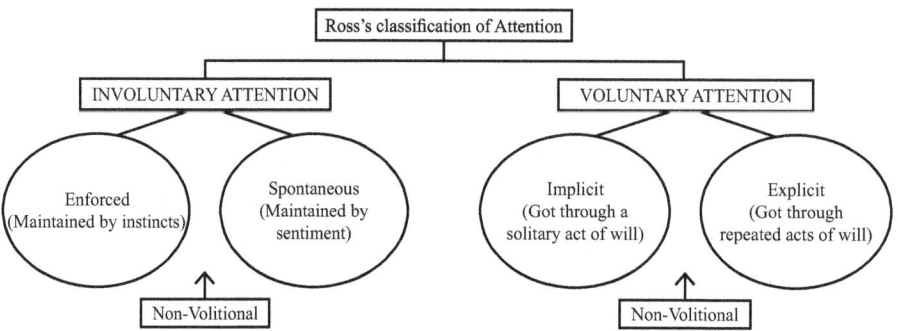

Determinants of Attention: (1) Nature of stimulus (2) Stimulus intensity and (3) Contrast, variety and change. (4) Stimulus repetition and (5) Stimulus movement. The above are external factors; there are internal factors also, and, they are: (1) Interest (2) Motives and (3) Mind-set.

If you are able to focus on more than one thing, you are said to possess a larger span-of-attention. How we comprehend the objects and situations/events in the external setting, which is the reality, is known as perception. You cannot retain attention with the same degree of intensity, as it is prone to fluctuate. Mason's Disc studies fluctuations in visual attention. A school-going child has to train his/her mind to focus his/her attention for a long time without interruption. It will ensure better results in learning.

B2: CHUNKING/ENCODING

Chunking is a process of recoding or reorganizing inputs in memory, which permits packaging a number of items into larger units. In Memory Organization Chunking plays a vital role. When inputs are organized effectively, it is possible to learn much more easily. The inputs are recoded into larger units known as chunks. "The fat girl saved the drowning boy" – in this sentence, the word 'fat' is bound to recall 'girl.' Likewise, if he recorded 'saved' he can also recall 'the drowning boy. But there is no guarantee that he can recall 'saved.' Is it chunked properly? You tell!

Encoding: Encoding refers to the code (i.e., the form) in which any message or item of information is stored with a facility to easy recall. Encoding plays an important role in recalling and recognizing any information instantly from memory.

B3: MEMORY CAPACITY

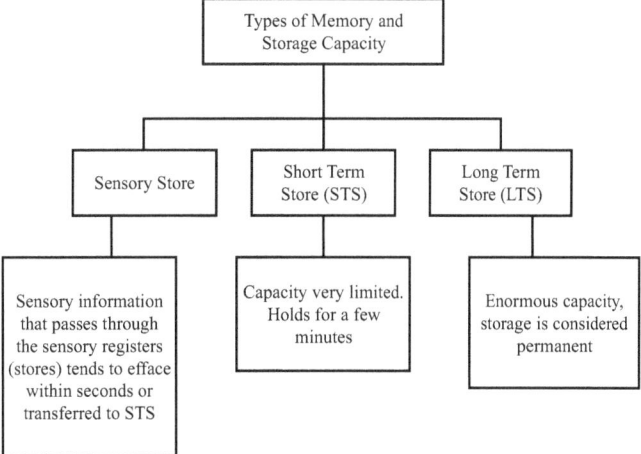

B4: MENTAL IMAGERY

It is an age-old saying that "we see it in our mind's eye." So visual memory is very important. Our memory system seems to retain some of the characteristics of our senses.

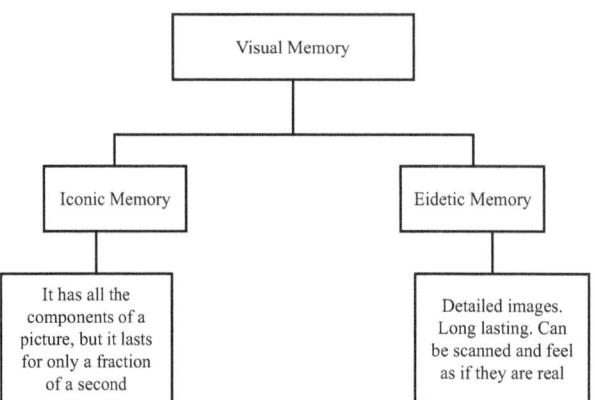

We perceive the world through images. However they are not photograph-like and hence our visual memory cannot be photographic-like. In Mental rotation, a letter, say "B," is shown in the normal way and then rotated at 60 or 120 or even in reverse format " ." The subject has to press a button once if the stimulus was normal, and twice if the reverse letter appeared. This exercise shows us that there is a separate visual memory system – says Cooper L.A. and Shepperd RN in "Memory and cognition."

Spatial Thinking is something we use when we want to know a possible short-cut between two places, or, when we are mentally involved in rearranging our library-room full of racks with books. Here we think in terms of pictures.

B5: ORGANIZATION OF LONG-TERM MEMORY

Sensory registers keep all inbound sensory information for fractions of seconds. It is believed that such sensory registers exist for all our senses.

Short-term memory holds good for a few minutes only. The capacity is very limited.

Both sensory registers as well as short-term memory provide a link to our immediate past. It is possible to transfer storage of sensory registers to short-term memory. Like wise whatever is stored in the short-term memory can be transferred to the long-term memory.

LONG-TERM MEMORY ORGANIZATION:

According to Ryburn, W.M, "Introduction to Educational Psychology" memory is: "…The power that we have to store our experiences, and to bring them into the field of our consciousness sometime after the experiences have occurred, is termed memory…" Storage and retrieval are very important. In long-term memory a huge storage of experiences is possible.

1. <u>Organization by phrases</u>: Recoding of items into larger chunks has taken place in the earlier years of a person's life. In such a scenario, an adult can make use of words that are a coherent whole, not a jumble of sounds. In sentences, a still higher unit of memory organization is associated.

2. <u>Organization by semantic categories</u>: In simple words it is like a shopping list. Defining category, followed by sub categories, such as: Vegetables – carrot, onion, potato, turnip, etc., followed by Fruits – apple, orange, grape, and pineapple. It is an organized set of defining items (Vegetables, fruits) followed by sub-categories (carrot under vegetables and apple under fruits).

3. <u>Organization by thematic content</u>: Understanding individual items of information by encoding them within the overall context, which facilitates easy recall at a later stage. This is organization by thematic content. Not only storing but also retrieval should be easy. If the context at the time of recall appears very near to that at the time of original encoding, retrieval become easy. This is referred to as <u>encoding specificity</u>.

B6: PROBLEM SOLVING

There are problems galore in every sphere of human activity. Every problem can be solved with a clear thinking approach. According to Skinner C.E – "Essentials of Educational Psychology": "Problem solving is a process of overcoming difficulties that appear to interfere with the attainment of a goal. It is a procedure of making adjustments in spite of interferences…" Example: I want to study the German language. How to learn the German language is my problem. Let us approach how to solve this problem schematically:

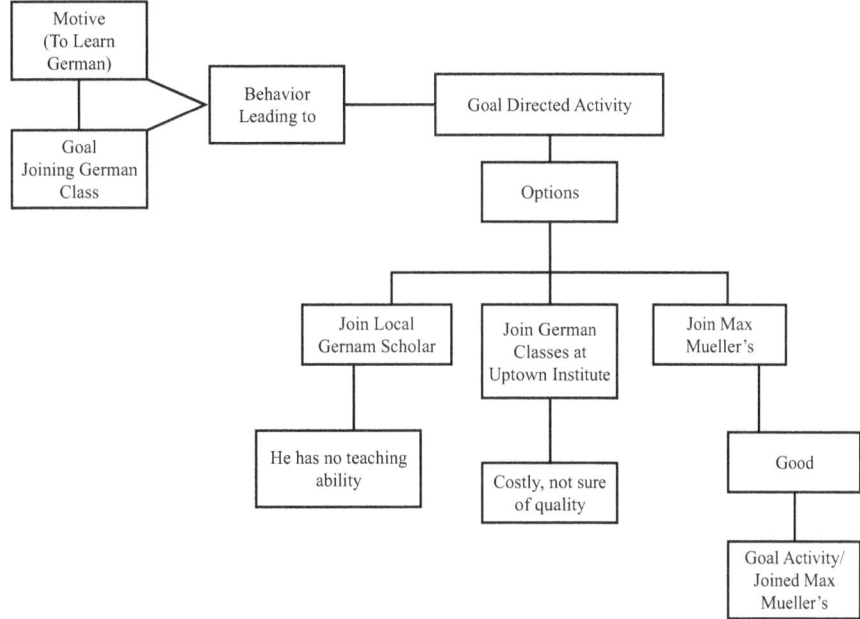

By joining Max Mueller's concepts, the problem is solved!

How to get problems solved? Bradford J.D and Stein BS, in their book "The ideal problem solver: A guide for improving thinking, learning and creativity" came up with a 5-stop problem-solving criteria® **I-D-E-A-L (IDEAL):**

I - **Identify the Problem.**
D - **Define the Problem.**
E - **Explore possible avenues/strategies.**
A - **Act on strategies.**
L - **Look back with a view to evaluate the situation.**

It is always better to put the actual problem in black and white.

(1)   What is the problem: Write down the problem.

(2)   What are the causes of the problem: Write down the possible causes that affected the problem.

(3)   What are the solutions: Write down possible solutions one by one;

(4)   What is the best solution? After considering all aspects, write down what is the best possible solution under the circumstances, and,

(5)   Act: Proceed to affect the solution.

B7: TRANSFER

Let us suppose you learn a particular task in a given situation. If this process of learning or training that particular task in that given situation leads to transfer of such learning or training to another task you have a transfer. If learning or training for the original task paves the way for learning the second task, you have a positive transfer. On the contrary, if learning or training for the original task hinders or obstructs learning the second task, you have a negative transfer. If there is no perceptible influence seen in the learning or training from one situation leading to another, you have a Zero transfer. There are quite a few theories on the transfer of learning or training: (1) Faculty Theory (a.k.a.: Theory of Mental discipline). Mental faculties like attention memory, reasoning and judgment can be trained and such training can be transferred automatically to other practical life situations. (2) Appreciation Theory of Transfer: In a learning situation, ideas and experiences are stored in one's unconscious mind, which is strengthened by repetition. Such strengthened storage of ideas or experiences can be automatically transferred to other learning situations. (3) Theory of identical elements or components: if there are identical elements involved in the original as well as the other situation, there is bound to be a transfer of learning or training. (4) Theory of generalization: Even though the elements present in both the situations are identical, transfer takes place in a generalized way, not on the basis of isolated facts related to such identical elements. (5) Transposition Theory: there should be a development and transposition of relevant insight for effecting a transfer from one learning situation to another. (6) Theory of Ideals: only ideals get transferred from one learning or training situation to another, and not generalization or isolated facts.

- (a) Transfer makes it possible for teacher and student to better teach and learn
- (b) It is in the hands of the teacher to maximize on possible effects.
- (c) The theory helps to active maximum possible transfer.

B8: TYPES OF MEMORY

One type of memory is called declarative memory, which is a form of long term memory. Declarative memory is long term memory of facts and events meant to be recalled and used. This type of memory is actually composed to two different factors: episodic memory and semantic memory. Episodic memory is the recall of autobiographical facts, such as dates, places and emotions. Episodic memory involves the specifics. This is what a person knows because of things that they have done. Semantic memory, on the other hand, involves general conceptual knowledge that a person has which wasn't necessarily acquired at any specific point in time. They know that a dog is a type of pet and a drill is a tool, and not the other way around. This type of information is not related to specific experiences.

Another type of memory is sensory memory. Sensory memory is memory which involves the five senses. Two types of sensory memory are iconic and echoic memory. Iconic memory is a type of visual sensory memory. It is the recall of something a person has seen for a brief period of time. For example, if someone shows you a picture and then you close your eyes and visualize it. Echoic memories have to do with auditory recall. It is the recall of something that a person has just heard, and is typically stored for only three to five seconds. For example, a person is watching TV and a friend asks them to do something. They stop the TV and ask their friend to repeat themselves, but realize that they remember what they said. This is echoic memory. Iconic and echoic memories are both short term memories. Iconic memories are generally stored for even less time than echoic memories.

A third type of memory is procedural memory. This is the recall of how to perform a specific task. It encompasses tasks that are performed frequently. Procedural memory is a type of long term memory, and conscious thought is not necessary to access it. For example, there have been people with amnesia who are able to sign their name even when they can't remember what it is.

 Behavior Perspective

The word 'behavior' is all encompassing of motor activities (swimming, walking, bowling), cognitive activities (thinking, reasoning, imagining), and, affective activities (feelings of happiness, sadness, anger).

C1: APPLICATIONS OF BEHAVIORISM

John B. Watson (1878-1950) propounded a new doctrine "Behaviorism" which was directly opposed to structuralism and functionalism. He states that since consciousness cannot be proved as it cannot be seen, touched or exhibited, i.e., it has no verifiable or quantifiable existence, it cannot be a factor in studying the psychology of behavior. Only, he opined, through overt and observable behavior, should any study be highlighted. What people do, and not a fistful of subjective notions, should be the basis of the study of behavioral theory.

By focusing on the observable and accountable behavior tendencies, behaviorism replaced the normal introspective norms with that of objective measures. Hereditary characters are not given prominence.

Children were observed not for their traits but for the role of environment in developing as well as modifying their behavior. This has a profound effect on education, training and rehabilitation programs, which were made to provide a child with the best possible learning situations and an excellent environment for healthy growth and development.

Unverifiable concepts like perception, sensation, emotions were out of the study of psychology and in their place concepts like response, stimulus, learning, and conditioning, habits were ushered in as incentives. Rewards and reinforcements replaced punishment as an inducement for the child to acquire desirable behavior patterns. Because of 'Behaviorism,' there has been a paradigm shift in the areas of learning and teaching ushering in concepts like 'programmed learning,' 'self-instructional programs' suited to individuals, computer- and internet-assisted teaching, etc.

Behaviorism is a learning theory which argues that learning is a result of observed behaviors, not of cognitive processes. The pattern of observing behaviors and learning is called conditioning. The two types of conditioning are classical conditioning and operant conditioning.

C2: BEHAVIORAL MODIFICATION PROGRAMS

This is a program that is systematic and structured to positively reinforce a child with desired positive behavior patterns achieved by inducements, incentives and rewards. Behavior Modification Programs for children in the age group of 3 to 11 years old are normally used to train a desired new behavior pattern. Such programs revolve around a structured and highly systematic program that has been found to be very effective. The goals fixed are growth and development oriented as well as age-appropriate to attain success. The goals set are observable using predefined yardsticks achievable within a predetermined time-frame. For smaller children between the ages of 3 to 5, the goals are oriented more towards ADL (Activities of Daily Living – bathing, grooming, toileting, etc.), peer and sibling relationships. Whatever goal is set, if achieved in full, the child is rewarded. A chart is prepared which correlates with each goal and the child receives stars, stickers or colors with a view to identify progress. Many nursery and primary schools use charts with distinct colors and this chart can be replicated in the home of the child for the parents to measure progress of the child. Preadolescents and adolescents do not require a colored chart linked with a goal and a reward for accomplishment. They are given behavioral contracts with goals that are 'psychodynamic' (e.g. showing respect to others, active participation in group activities, politely talking to others, etc.). When goals are achieved, instead of stars/stickers, a checkmark indicating accomplishment of goal is placed after each goal.

C3: CLASSICAL CONDITIONING

Ivan Petrovich Pavlov, a Russian Nobel Laureate (for work on digestion) is credited with the classical conditioning theory. This theory postulates 'learning' as 'habit' formation, which relies on principles of association and substitution. It normally is a stimulus-response sort of learning in which in the place of a natural stimulus, such as food, an artificial stimulus such as the sound of a bell or the sight of a light of distinct colors, etc., are sure to produce a natural response. When both natural as well as artificial stimuli are carried together, many times, there is bound to be a conditioned response to the situation. If the natural stimuli, is substituted with the artificial stimuli after sometime, it is likely to produce the same response as the natural stimuli would have evoked.

In Pavlov's famous dog experiment, he would ring a bell and then feed the dogs. Initially, the dogs would salivate when given food, however over time the dogs began to salivate at the sound of the bell. Classical conditioning describes a link between a stimulus and a response in which a person or animal associates or substitutes a neutral stimulus, such as the bell, with the actual stimulus, the food. Many reflexive reactions, such as a person covering their eyes when something flies in front of their face, or salivating at the smell of their favorite food, can be explained through classical conditioning.

John Watson (1878-1958) who had given us "behaviorism," supported Pavlov's thinking in so far as conditioned responses go. In an experiment, a child who was afraid of rabbits was left in a room where a rabbit was sitting at a great distance. Slowly the distance was reduced and one day the rabbit was sitting on the table when the child was eating. Next, it was placed on the child's lap while he was eating. The association of a rabbit nearby while eating ensured the child would have no fear of rabbits and the child started playing with it. This is a case of simple conditioning in which a child who was afraid of rabbits, gradually overcame the fear and started playing with what he once feared!

C4: COGNITIVE LEARNING THEORY

Learning theories can be broadly clarified into two major groups: (1) Behaviorists Theories (a.k.a. – Connectionists' Theories) and, (2) Cognitive Theories. Behaviorists' theories study learning as an association or link between stimulus and the response it begets. On the other hand cognitive theories rely on cognitive factors such as reasoning, purpose, memory, insight, understanding, etc. Theories that can be classified under cognitive learning are:

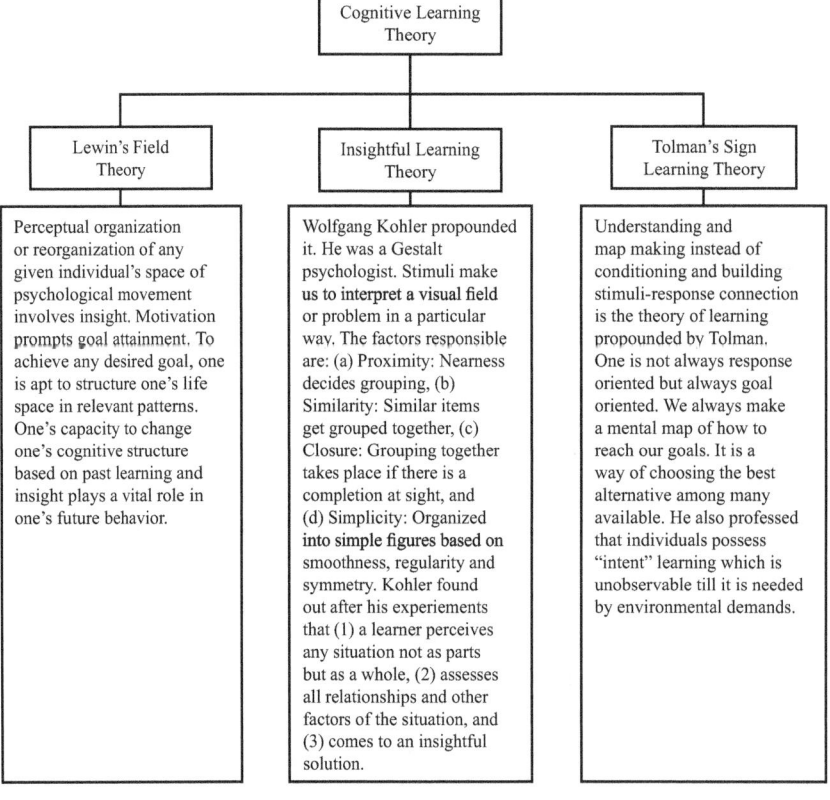

C5: LAW OF EFFECT, OPERANT CONDITIONING, PREMACK PRINCIPLE, SCHEDULES OF REINFORCEMENT AND TOKEN ECONOMIES

Another theory which goes along with the idea of conditioning is Edward Thorndike's Law of Effect. The Law of Effect states that if a situation or action produces a positive outcome or feeling. it is more likely to be repeated. If a situation or action produces a negative outcome or feeling, it will become less likely to be repeated. According to Thorndike "The Law of Effect" can be stated thus: "…When a modifiable connection between stimulus and response is made and is accompanied or followed by a satisfying state of affairs, that connection's strength is increased. When made and accompanied or followed by an annoying state of affairs, its strength is decreased…" to put it in simple terms, if a response is followed by a reward, the response to a stimulus gets strengthened.

It is weakened if the response does not attract a reward. B.P. Skinner is credited with "operant conditioning" theory. It is a form of learning in which a "reinforcement" (let us say a cookie) is given time and again to the animal under study only if, or when, the animal performs the instrumental response (let us say hitting a red button). As long as it did not perform the hitting the red button act, the animal would not get the cookie. It highlights the relationship between response and reinforcement.

The Premack principle is a system which uses operant conditioning to make less probable actions more likely to occur by using more probable actions as reinforcers. For example, most children do not like doing laundry, making it the less probable action. However, most children do enjoy watching television, making it the more probable action. If a mother tells her children that they can watch television if they do the laundry, she is using the Premack principle, with the television being the reinforcer.

Schedules of reinforcement was a plan organized by Skinner for conditioning 'operant behavior' of the organism. Some of the schedules are: (1) Continuous reinforcement schedules: reward for every correct response. (2) Fixed interval reinforcement schedule: reward is given for the correct response only after a fixed interval of time. (3) Fixed ratio reinforcement schedule: reward is given only after performing a fixed number of responses (let us say; a cat gets a cookie only after it presses the red button at least 5 times). (4) Variable reinforcement schedule: reinforcement is given (a) at varying time intervals, and/or, (b) after varying number of responses. Here rewards are given irregularly so much so there is an element of unpredictableness, which is bound to motivate.

Behavior modification objective is always aimed at eliminating undesirable behavior patterns. The other objective, more especially in a hospital setting, is to get patients to do certain desirable acts. Operant behavior therapists seek to provide an appropriate reinforcement to motivate patients to do desirable acts. Chronic patients or patients declared to be at the end of their life-span, are given 'tokens' to be exchanged for desirable items within a given hospital situation (example – exchanging the token for snacks, or cookies, etc.). The token has to be earned by following certain observable ward chores, (being neatly dressed, bathing, talking to other people in a nice way, etc., can also be tasks). This has nothing to do with healing. But it ensures a congenial ward atmosphere.

Operant conditioning is a type of conditioning in which a person associates an action with a consequence. The main difference between operant conditioning and classical conditioning is that classical conditioning works more to explain reflexive or unconscious reactions, whereas operant conditioning works to explain elective actions and reactions. For example, a student will wish to do well in school because it brings the consequence of good grades and parental approval. Studies have shown that even infants can be taught certain behaviors using operant conditioning. When operant conditioning is used to shift an existing response to a target response it is called shaping.

Operant conditioning depends upon reinforcers to as a method of learning. A reinforcer is anything which makes a behavior more likely to reoccur. Reinforcers can be positive or negative. A positive reinforcer is when something pleasant is used to make a behavior more likely. Parents paying their children for good grades or a person giving their pet a treat for doing a trick are both examples of positive reinforcers. A negative reinforcer is when something unpleasant is removed from a situation. For example, if a student studies more they are less anxious. The anxiety is an unpleasant feeling which is removed as a result of studying, and therefore studying is a form of negative reinforcement. Conditioning can also occur using punishments, which instead of making a behavior more likely to reoccur, attempt to make it less likely to reoccur. Like reinforcers, punishments can be both positive (if something unpleasant is introduced) and negative (if something pleasant is removed).

Development

D1: ADOLESCENCE

Adolescence is derived from a Latin root which literally means "Growing up." It is the period when a child grows and develops into adulthood. Adolescence is reckoned as the ages between 13 to 17 or 18 years (normally from the onset of puberty to maturity). During this stage a certain amount of inner turmoil takes place. It is the transition time in an individual from childhood to adulthood. During this period one evolves into a mature adult, reaching levels of maturity in physical, mental, emotional and social spheres. Compared to animals the path of growth and development towards maturity is rather slow. Animals mature faster!

There is a traditional view of adolescence as being a stage where inner turmoil and emotional stress are predominant. This view was subscribed to by writers like Goethe. Sigmund Freud also endorsed this view. According to Freud, Adolescence was a stage of conflict as during that period sex urges forcefully came to the fore, which were repressed during the Oedipal complex conflict period. Whatever unconscious conditioning has existed previously, the mind rebels against it freely now. The modern writers feel that turbulence need not necessarily be the underlying motive of adolescence as, largely, emotional disturbances depend on the social and cultural handling of the turbulence. However, during adolescence an individual recognizes the need for a separate identity in order to establish an independent world of his/her own.

D2: COGNITIVE DEVELOPMENT

In human growth and development, the following points that are all encompassing need study: (1) motor development (attaining motor skills), (2) cognitive development (intellectual functioning), and (3) social development (dealing with others). A child not only grows physically, but also grows mentally. A child perceives, understands it, recollects and talks about it. This growth, which is solely intellectual, escorting a child in all its developmental activities from infancy to adulthood, is known as <u>cognitive development</u>. A child's cognitive development is analogous to a typist who starts from letter typing to high speed typing.

According to Jean Piaget (1896-1980), a Swiss psychologist, all human beings pass through a process of cognitive development. The current thinking is that cognitive development can be seen as a change in information processing. Increased mental ability is an account of acquisitions of larger chunks of different strategies for thinking and recalling.

The visual cliff was an experiment designed to test the age at which infants develop depth perception. The idea was to create the illusion that there was a cliff present, and see if the infant would still climb over the area. The setup was to have an elevated area, with half of it having a black and white checkered pattern and the other half glass. Underneath the glass (at floor level) the black and white checkered pattern continued. The criticism of the experiment was that in a way it could be testing whether or not the infant had an understanding of the consequences of going over the ledge, just as much as it tested whether or not they saw it.

D3: GENDER IDENTITY/SEX ROLES

Speaking biologically, Gender identity is simple enough. A human cell comprises of 46 pairs of chromosomes, 23 pairs each from male (father) and female (mother). Females have only "X" Chromosome pairs, while Males do have one pair comprising of an "X" and a "Y" chromosome. If all 23 pairs of chromosomes of a male are "XX," the gender identity is "Female" and if 22 pairs of chromosomes of a male are "XX" and the 23rd pair is "XY," then the gender identity is "Male." Psychologically this points out:

(1) Gender identity (our intrinsic feeling as to whatever we are, male or female)

(2) Gender Role (the external behavior pattern that is relevant for each sex as deemed appropriate by the culture to which one belongs), and

(3) Sexual orientation (liking a partner, normally from the opposite sex).

These three together define an individual's "social" existence. Social factors essentially fashion our sense of being a woman or man and this gradually shapes up our behavior. According to Sigmund Freud, the basic mechanism is identification. The child generally takes on his/her father or mother as role model, which, according to Freud, is the end result of the Oedipus complex conflict. According to the social learning theory a child behaves in a sex-appropriate way according to the rewards or punishments he/she knows, he/she gets. To find an appropriate sex-behavior, a child, if he is a male, imitates his father and if she is a female, imitates her mother. Cognitive development theory suggests that a child possesses a vague idea of what a female or male means and gains comprehension with more exposure to reality.

D4: LANGUAGE ACQUISITION

Language learning depends on (1) heredity and (2) environment. Language learning is something special; it is not just like acquiring any other skills. Let us see what a child achieves in the first 30 months of existence;

AGE	LINGUISTIC ACHIEVEMENT
1st year of life	Prespeech – cooing, gestures
by 12 months	Holophrase – single words (mommy)
by 18th months	Telegraphic Speech – two word utterances
2-2/12 yrs	Multi-word sentences
2/1/2-4 yrs	Progressively more complex

Source: "Biological foundations of language"-E.H. Lenneberg 1967: pp. 128-30. A language is (a) highly organized, and (b) creative sound, meaning and grammar are used according to the organized principles of a given language to create any number of new sentences. These structural principles are to be obeyed in order to speak and make others understand the language. Every sentence consists of phrase/phrases, which consist of word/words, which again consist of morpheme. At the root level there is a group of phonemes; each language uses less than fifty basic sounds (phonemes) out of which all the words in any given language are constructed.

Hereditary characteristics passed through genes as well as environment play an important role in language learning. Imitation, reinforcement and correction – these are mostly principles in thinking and perception but play no significant part in language learning. Children are pre-equipped to create and answer to language sounds. But they learn to overlook sound distinctions that do not matter. They respond well to <u>mothers</u> (A term used for speech pattern that mothers or other grown-ups normally use when talking to infants), which indicates sound cues do aid the baby to identify the <u>sentence</u> as a speech unit.

D5: MENTAL HEALTH

What is Mental Health? And, what is Mental Disorder? The distinction between Mental Health and Mental Disorder can be seen in the following illustration.

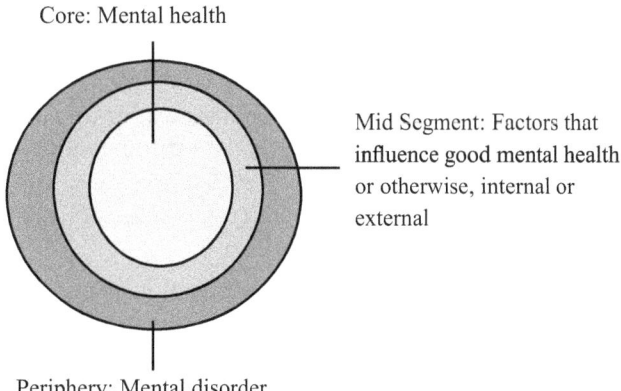

This Mental Health – Mental Disorder continuously changes perennially in accordance with developments in internal and external factors. Even the healthiest person, mentally, may have a few symptoms of dysfunction. Likewise, a person with mental disorder may also show layers of mental health. There is no proper definition for mental health, at least so far. So far Mental Health has been illustrated only through linear paradigms. Erikson. E, in his wonderful book "Childhood in Society," states: ."..that genetics and environmental experiences, which begin with conception and continue throughout life, determine the person's personality and his or her mentally healthy or destructive responses to the world…" The following factors influence one's Mental

Health: (1) heredity (2) family (3) culture (4) sub-culture (5) value systems, (6) belief systems, and (7) self-perception.

D6: MORAL DEVELOPMENT

The development of moral judgment/reasoning is a process of thinking about what is right and what is wrong in a given situation. The development of moral thinking and judgment was studied by Jean Piaget, Lawrence Kolberg, Carol Gilligare and Robert Coles, and they have come up with their own theories. According to Piaget, children before age five to six are somewhat egocentric as they are unable to see the world from any other angle except their own. This egocentric aspect rubs off when the child is making a moral judgment. Lawrence Kolberg postulated his own theory of moral development. According to him there are successive stages of moral development. Kolberg's stages of moral development are given below.

Kohlberg's Theory of Moral Development

Level 1: Preconventional Morality

Stage 1: Punishment and obedience phase. Whether you will be punished or not determines what is moral or not. For example, you don't speed when driving the car because you know that you might get a ticket-a negative sanction from an authority figure.

Stage 2: A person becomes aware of two different viewpoints. You don't speed while driving a car because you want the lower rates on car insurance that you will get having no tickets on your record.

Level 2: Conventional Morality

Stage 3: You do what is right in order to gain status or approval from other people or society. For example, you don't get speeding tickets while driving because in your circle of friends that would make you appear irresponsible, therefore lowering your social status.

Stage 4: A person abides by the law because they think that law is a higher order. It is their duty as a responsible citizen to not speed. This type of person would not run a red light in a deserted intersection even if he had been waiting five minutes. They believe that laws cannot be broken under any circumstance.

Level 3: Postconventional Morality

Stage 5: A person is concerned with how their action might affect society, i.e., "I'm not going to speed because I might get into an accident and injure someone."

Stage 6: A person makes decisions according to his or her conscience. Not many, if any, people get to this stage. Kohlberg believed that you went through stages one at a time and could not skip them. According to both Kohlberg and Piaget, the most immature reason to do something is to avoid punishment.

D7: SCHOOL READINESS

Reasoning is an important skill that we humans possess. A successful person has good reasoning skills. Children should be prepared in the right way at every step to reason according to their age group. The actual stages are given below:

1. <u>Sensorimotor stage: (Birth to 2 years of age)</u>:

   Understands only people in direct contact and immediate environment. They do not think. Only touching, listening, seeing and perhaps sucking are what they understand. Cuddling and coddling are important.

2. <u>The pre-reasoning stage: (2 years of age to 7 yrs.)</u>:

   Using symbols and recognizing them develops. From age 3, it is time for Pre-school readiness. Can recite rhymes, and numbers. Normally, in kindergarten even the walls have a lot of symbols, drawings, photos, graphics, etc.

3. <u>The concrete reasoning stage: (Age 7 to 12 yrs.)</u>:

   Whatever reasoning abilities were developed previously remain concrete. Children understand numbers and rhymes. Participate in team games, role-playing, etc. Ready for Elementary level classes. From here on students are trained to go further into middle and upper, secondary levels.

4. <u>The formal reasoning stage: (Age above 12 yrs.)</u>:

   They now know how to think, know what a 'concept' is, and understand general principles of reasoning. Capable of solving theoretical or hypothetical problems through necessary rules.

D8: SOCIAL DEVELOPMENT

We can safety state that Social Development is a process through which children learn the behavior patterns they need to internalize in order to survive and function in society. The appropriate behaviors are the end results of frequent and repeated interactions in their environment. During the process of socialization a child is raised within a sub-culture – culture combined, all the while acquiring the distinct characteristics of it. A child's socialization starts with the first human bond the child has occasion to form, his/her attachment to his/her mother. This is the most comforting bond a child receives. When the child is separated even for a few hours from this experienced bond, separation anxiety is felt. There are the "Social Learning Theory," which is emphatic about models, and the "Cognitive Development Theory," which relies on "understanding" as opposed to "imitation." The most important aspect in a child's social development is the atmosphere available in the home circuit. Whether the home thrives on "autocratic," "permissive" or "authoritative-reciprocal" patterns of child reasoning is important.

Sigmund Freud was the first to device a "psychosexual" development theory. According to him adult problems emanate to childhood trauma-there are Oral (id) Anal (ego), Phallic (superego) and Latency Genital stages in a Child's social development.

James Marcia is known for developing a theory of identity development known as the Identity Status Theory. Marcia worked under Erik Erikson, and his Identity Status Theory takes a closer look at development during youth. Marcia identifies four different stages that occur as an individual strives to develop their own identity. Although it is not necessary for everyone to pass through each stage, they do follow a spectrum as an identity becomes more solidified. The four stages that Marcia identified are identity diffusion, identity foreclosure, identity moratorium, and identity achievement. Each stage is characterized by different levels of identity exploration and commitment.

The identity diffusion stage is characterized by a lack of independence. Because youth have not needed to make important life decisions, they haven't truly determined their own identity. In other words, there are low levels of both exploration and commitment. The second stage, identity foreclosure, occurs as a youth begins to make decisions about their future, but without questioning their values and beliefs. In other words, identity foreclosure involves a high level of commitment (being willing to make educational and work decisions) but low levels of exploration. As youth begin to question the values that they have been taught and explore their own beliefs, they move into the identity moratorium stage. In this stage individuals become less willing to make commitments, and begin exploring the variety of options available to them. This stage is basically one of identity crisis. Following this period of crises is a stage of achievement. The identity achievement stage is characterized by high levels of both exploration and commitment. Youth are able to both discover new paths and ideas, but also to commit to a course of action based on them. This allows for healthy behaviors of continued growth and progression.

Erik Erikson was a psychoanalyst who documented stages of emotional growth in regards to human babies. Each stage has different needs and lessons to be learned. If the child or infant does not learn a specific lesson, he may have a harder time in life down the road. For example, if a baby is crying constantly and is not taken care of, or if they are ignored, they can come to feel mistrust towards others. Another example is found in the young adult stage. The young adult must deal with either being intimate with someone or dealing with feeling isolated. According to Erickson, the most important thing is the development of trust.

Infant *Trust vs. Mistrust*
Infants gain trust and confidence from their caregivers. If those caregivers are warm and responsive then they will know that the world is good. Mistrust occurs from being handled poorly and inattentiveness on the part of the caregiver.

Toddler *Autonomy vs. Shame and Doubt*
Children want to make their own decisions. Autonomy is when the parents give the child that necessary free reign over their choices.

Preschooler *Initiative vs. Guilt*
Children play at different roles. They can try their hand at being a princess or a mother or father to their dolls. Ever wonder why children at this age love dress-up clothes?

School-Age Child *Industry vs. Inferiority*
Children learn to work with others.

Adolescent *Identity vs. Role Confusion*
This is the standard teen question: "Who am I?"

Young Adult *Intimacy vs. Isolation*
Young adults seek emotional ties with others. Because of earlier trust situations (divorce of parents, for example), some young adults are unable to form attachments and this leaves them isolated.

Middle-Age Adult *Generativity vs. Stagnation*
Generativity means giving to the next generation. Those that do not do these things feel unhappy.

Old Age *Ego integrity vs. Despair*
In this stage, people think about what they have done with their life. Integrity comes from achieving what one wanted in life. Despair results in fear of death for those that are unhappy with their past.

Sullivan suggests that social development arises on account of interpersonal relationships in each stage or era of development of a child. Piaget's Cognitive Theory and Kohlberg's Moral Development Theory were studied in an earlier Building Block.

Erikson's Theory of Psychosocial Development identifies eight stages through which people progress as they age. Each stage is characterized by either developing a characteristic or not. According to his model, adolescents are in the identity role vs. role confusion stage. James Marcia expanded this model by claiming that it was a simple conflict between developing an identity or not. He argued that the stage was characterized by the presence or absence two factors: conflict and commitment. Conflict describes a time when a person must evaluate their beliefs, and is generally followed by commitment (to either change them or hold to them). Four different combinations emerge using these factors and Marcia labeled them identity diffusion, identity foreclosure, identity moratorium and identity achievement. It is important to remember that these descriptions are not stages, they are more like statuses.

Identity diffusion describes a state where a person experiences no conflict and makes no commitments. They just go along with their lives accepting what they are told but with no real dedication to it. This type of person will have not had to deal with great conflict in their lives, but their identity will be "diffused," vague and undefined.

Identity foreclosure occurs when a person makes a commitment but there has been no crisis. He called it foreclosure to suggest that the commitment has been made too soon. When foreclosure occurs a person will have no personal basis for their beliefs because they will have accepted wholesale the things that they have been told.

Identity moratorium occurs when a person is in crisis but hasn't made a commitment. For example, if a person's parents run a restaurant in a small town and intend to hand it down to them one day. However, this person wants to be an actor on Broadway instead, so they will experience conflict. If they persist in making no commitments to either their parents or their dreams, and instead are just angry or sad all of the time, it is moratorium.

Identity achievement describes the state in which a person has both experienced conflict and made a commitment. This is the hoped for status. A person will have a defined believe system and decided on path. They will have developed their identity.

D9: LEARNING THEORIES

Lev Vygotsky developed the theory of social development to describe how and why children learn. He stated that every function in the child's development appears twice; first between people and then inside the child. There were three elements to his theory. The first element is the idea that social interaction facilitates cognitive improvement. In other words, the child's interaction with other people and their environment occurs before learning. The second aspect is the presence of a More Knowledgeable Other (MKO). This person is more knowledgeable than the child is in a specific area. It could be a parent, teacher, coach, friend, or even a computer. The third element is the Zone of Proximal Development (ZPD). This describes the fact that there is a gap between what the child can do with help, and what they can do on their own. When the child recognizes this gap, they will work to close it. When this occurs, they have learned.

Assimilation and accommodation are two distinct, but often complimentary, processes of learning and adaptation. Assimilation occurs when new information is encountered and viewed in terms of what is already known. In other words, it is input into the brain without changing existing ideas. Accommodation is when information is encountered and input into the brain, and the brain must accommodate or adapt to the new information. This occurs when information is encountered that contradicts preexisting ideas.

Elaboration is a learning theory which is primarily based on the idea of association. It focuses on laying out fundamental concepts and then building on them. It also involves a lot of review in an attempt to make the learner associate the more complex topics with the basic ones.

Edwin Guthrie was a psychologist known for developing the contiguity theory. This theory claims that learning occurs as a result of experience and habit-formation. Guthrie essentially argued that a set of occurrences would elicit a response from an individual. From that point onward, that response would be associated in their mind with those occurrences, and a habit will have been formed. Guthrie believed that action was required for learning to occur. According to Guthrie's contiguity theory, it is irrelevant how many times the behavior has been previously performed.

Once the habit has been formed then an individual's response will be the same regardless of whether the conditioning is repeated. It is possible that once a habit has been formed it can be overcome, but this takes a process of relearning a new response. According to Guthrie this can be accomplished in three ways. First, if the subject is placed in a situation where they are unable to respond in their conditioned manner and must learn a new behavior. Second, if the subject becomes too tired or exhausted to respond in their normal manner. The final reconditioning method is if the stimulus is introduced so faintly that the subject becomes desensitized to it.

D10: MEMORY

Retroactive inhibition and proactive inhibition are two types of interference theory. Interference theory describes how learning new information has an effect on memory loss as a result of competition between information.

Proactive inhibition is when old memory is lost due to new memory gained, and is especially true in situations where the new memory and old memory are similar. For example, many experiments have been done where two groups of people are asked to memorize a list of words. The first group is then asked to memorize a second list while the first group is asked to perform an unrelated task (meant to keep them from consciously working on remembering the list). The two groups are then asked to recall the list. Typically, the group which had to memorize two lists has worse recall.

Retroactive inhibition is just the opposite. This is when old information interferes with the learning of new information. This is also true when the information is in the same area. For example, if a person has had the same credit card number for years, but is issued a new number because their account is compromised, they generally have a more difficult time learning the new number because they are so used to the old number.

D11: MEASURING INTELLIGENCE

Charles Spearman proposed the idea of a universal intelligence factor which he called the general intelligence factor, or g. Technically, he believed that intelligence was composed of two intellectual areas – a general cognitive ability and aptitudes in specific areas. However, he placed importance on the existence of a general factor. Spearman observed a positive correlation in testing scores. In other words, generally if a person did well in one subject, they did well in other subjects too. Because of this, he believed that there it was possible to determine a quantity describing each person's intelligence. His work became the basis for later IQ testing.

After Spearman proposed his idea of a universal intelligence factor, it became the most accepted model. However, Louis L. Thurstone believed that intelligence could not be narrowed down to a specific factor, and believed that there were multiple factors which contributed to intelligence which Spearman's research did not account for. His Theory of Primary Mental Abilities set forth seven abilities which he believed existed. They are word fluency, verbal comprehension, spatial visualization, number ability, associative memory, reasoning and perceptual speed. His work laid the groundwork for later theorists such as Gardner and Sternberg to propose their own multiple factor models.

Howard Gardner developed a model of multiple intelligences which challenges the idea that everyone has the same ability to learn. According to Gardner's model, there are different types of intelligence, and everyone excels in different areas. The seven intelligences are visual-spatial, bodily-kinesthetic, musical, interpersonal, intrapersonal, linguistic and logical-mathematical. A person can have any combination of strengths and weaknesses of the seven categories.

The visual-spatial intelligence describes people who are aware of their environment and think in terms of physical space. For example, they like art and might to jigsaw puzzles. They like video games, movies and other electronics. When they look in a textbook they make more sense of the graphs and visuals than the text.

The bodily-kinesthetic intelligence describes people who are active and aware of themselves. They like physical activity and hands on learning. These people communicate well through body language.

The musical intelligence describes people who love music, but it also extends to sounds in the environment. They like musical instruments, radios or multimedia, and may learn better by writing songs or using rhythm to help them memorize.

The interpersonal intelligence describes people who like to interact with others. They are outgoing, have many friends and prefer group activities to working alone. Unlike the stereotype of a chatty student who often disrupts the class, this type of person truly does learn and understand better when they work in a group.

The intrapersonal intelligence describes people who understand their own interests, needs and goals. They tend to be shy, but are smart and intuitive. They suffer in a group setting but flourish when left to independent study and quiet time.

The linguistic intelligence is the ability to use words effectively. This is the intelligence that Gardner believed was too overemphasized in society, along with the logical-mathematical intelligence. This type of person does well at speaking, reading text and word games. They like to read and listen to lectures.

The logical-mathematical intelligence describes people who like calculating and reasoning. They may like puzzles, patterns and abstract concepts. They ask questions and do well at following sets of instructions with understood results. They need to learn concepts before they can see the details of things.

Robert J Sternberg developed his triarchic model of intelligence in part as a criticism of the standard IQ test. He believed that the test was fundamentally flawed because it focused on a person's ability to perform cognitive processes. His triarchic model defines three different aspects of intelligence: analytical (or componential), creative (or experiential) and practical (or contextual). The analytical aspect does focus of the traditional cognitive ability of a person. It involves verbal, mathematical and logical skills. Basically, the analytical aspect is the ability to understand universal concepts. The creative aspect focuses on a person's ability to interact with their environment. It involves creativity, the ability to deal with new or innovative situations and divergent thinking. The creative aspect is a person's ability to come up with their own ideas. The final aspect, practical, involves a person's ability to apply their knowledge to real world situations.

D12: CONVERGENT THINKING

Guilford was an American psychologist who studied how different people can come up with different answers to the same situations. It was Guilford who first proposed the idea of convergent and divergent thinking. Convergent thinking is the type of thinking that people typically think of when it comes to school settings. It is finding the one most correct answer as quickly and accurately as possible. Convergent thinkers focus on logical patterns, and accumulating knowledge that will apply to future situations. Divergent thinkers are the more creative types. They look for new and innovative solutions for problems. They are resourceful and do flourish in situations with many possibilities.

Ellis Paul Torrance is known for his work in trying to quantify creativity. He built upon Guilford's theory of divergent thinking and created a test designed to measure creative abilities on a basis of fluency (the number of responses), flexibility (the number of categories the responses fell into), originality (determined by statistical rarity of the response) and elaboration (the amount of detail). His test is known as the Torrance Tests of Creative Thinking.

D13: CAROL GILLIGAN AND MORAL DEVELOPMENT

Carol Gilligan was born in New York in 1936. She studied clinical psychology and eventually went on to teach at Harvard and work closely in research with Erik Erikson and Lawrence Kohlberg-two renowned psychological theorists. Working closely with these men, Gilligan began to feel that their moral theories were biased against women, and she developed her own theory of moral development. Gilligan noted that women were not less moral than men (as Erikson and Kohlberg's theories both insinuated), but rather they have a different moral code. Gilligan argues that men are more prone to consider ethics in terms of justice. Principles such as fairness, independence, and justice are very important. On the other hand, Gilligan notes that women are typically more prone to view morality through the lens of ethics of care. With this theory self-sacrifice, service, relationships, and love are all important factors in determining morality.

Gilligan also goes on to describe three different stages through which morality develops in women: pre-conventional, conventional, and post-conventional. The pre-conventional stage describes childhood. In this stage, both men and women are primarily focused on themselves. It is the "selfish" stage. According to Gilligan this serves a survival function. Children transition from the pre-conventional stage into the conventional stage of morality following childhood. This stage is characterized by a rather different goal: the desire to serve others. This is why the mother role comes naturally to women – self-sacrifice is an important moral characteristic. Finally, in the postconventional stage there is a confident balance between selfishness and self-sacrifice. A woman is able to confidently focus on others, without being a detriment to herself. The main goal is to see that no harm comes to others or self.

Motivation

The motivation of individuals depends on the strengths of their motives. (Motives→needs, wants, drives or impulses within an individual). Motives arouse and sustain activity and determine the general direction of an individual's behavior. In other words, motives are the mainsprings of action. Successful motivation is nothing but providing an environment in which appropriate incentives (goals, rewards) are available for need satisfaction. According to Sigmund Freud, motivation of most individuals likens that of an iceberg.

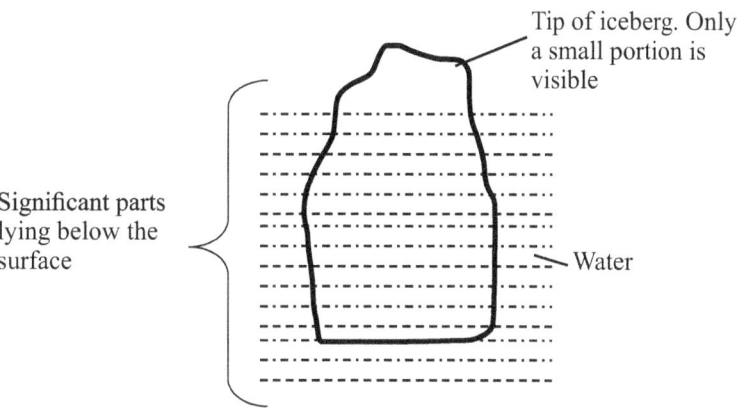

Motivation - Iceberg

From the illustration one can see that a significant portion of human motivation lies in the water below the surface and this portion is not readily evident to the individual. These are subconscious motives, which are not easily felt by individuals.

E1: ACHIEVEMENT MOTIVATION – ANXIETY/STRESS

David C. McClelland did research on achievement motivation. He found that the need for achievement is a distinct human motive that can be distinguished from other needs. This need is a basic and natural need. According to Atkinson J.W, and Feather N.T – "A Theory of Achievement Motivation," "…the achievement motive is conceived as a latent disposition which is manifested in overt striving only when the individual perceives performance as instrumental to a sense of personal accomplishment…" Only achievement motivation makes people strive for excellence in their chosen field. Children normally acquire achievement motives from their parents. A child who was brought up in a free, fair and most congenial atmosphere of family life, which represents democratic as against autocratic values, given full freedom to act, is most like to develop an achievement-oriented attitude; and with this attitude strengthening over the years, he is bound to go for excellence in whatever he does.

Anxiety/Stress: It is an emotional state of mind similar to fear. Sigmund Freud was of the view that many a mental illness emanates from anxiety and one's efforts to come out of it by unconscious means. A very good definition was given by Katherine M. Fortinash, and, Patricia A. Holoday – in their wonderful book "Psychiatric Mental Health Nursing," "…A vague, subjective, nonspecific feeling of uneasiness, tension, apprehension, and sometimes dread or pending doom occurs as a result of a threat to one's biologic, psychologic, or social integrity arising from external influences. A universal experience and an integral part of human existence…"

In the same book, the same authors have given a wonderful definition for stress: "… A term that refers to both a stimulus and a response. It can denote a non-specific response of the body to any demand placed on it, whether the causal event is negative (a painful experience) or positive (a happy occasion). (2) A state produced by a change in the environment that is perceived as challenging, threatening, or damaging to the person's dynamic equilibrium. (3) The wear and tear on the body over time. (4) Psychologic stress has been defined as all processes, whether originating in the external environment or within the person, that demand a mental appraisal of the event before the involvement or activation of any other system.…"

E2: LOCUS OF CONTROL/ATTRIBUTION THEORY; LEARNED HELPLESSNESS, INTRINSIC MOTIVATION

There are many aspects to personality and "locus of control" is a very important aspect. There are "internal locus of control" and "external locus of control" within the personality. Anyone having "internal locus of control" believes that they are in good control of their own destiny. Those with "external locus of control" always perceive that they do not have any control whatsoever over their destiny and therefore think that their behavior patterns have no say on the outcome.

Attribution theory tries to find out why a person behaved the way he did – is it possible to assess the causes and attribute it to situational factors or draw inference as to any internal dispositional qualities.

Learned helplessness or secondary locus of control tells us that persons with "external locus of control" (persons have no control over their destiny and as a consequence think that their behavior patterns have no say on the outcome) always believe in their helplessness. What we perceive is reality. If a person believes or perceives that the situation in which he/she is placed is uncontrollable, this state is likely to lead to helplessness, apathy, powerlessness and ultimately to depression.

Intrinsic motivation refers to an inner state of mind to achieve a goal. It is a native (inborn) tendency always present inside an individual to persuade or inspire him for action for satisfying basic needs or to attain any specific need.

E3: THEORIES OF MOTIVATION

1. McDougall's Theory of Instinct is as follows "…The human mind has certain innate or inherited tendencies which are the essential springs or motive power of all thoughts and actions, whether individual or collective and are the basis from which the character and will of individuals and of nations are gradually developed under the guidance of intellectual faculties…" W. McDougall – Social Psychology

– listed 14 instincts and said that each of these instincts is accompanied by a certain particular emotional disposition. He claimed that behavior is instinctive and has the following three aspects to it. (1) Knowing (cognition) (2) Feeling (affection) and,

(3) Doing (conation).

2. Hull's Drive Reduction Theory was propounded by Clark Leonard Hull (Principles of Behavior). According to him only biological drives (Thirst, hunger, sex, etc.) are accountable for sustaining the primary responses. He felt that the above creates a mounting tension in the mind, which willy-nilly has to find a solution for reduction of such built up tension. According to W.B. Cannon, our body system always strives to maintain balance and works towards optimum levels of functioning. He coined the system as "home-ostasis." (The maintaining of blood-pressure levels, body-temperature, etc., within norms.)

3. Sigmund Freud's Psycho-analytic Theory of Motivation. Emphasizes role of 'instincts' as the main troublemaker of all human activities, particularly two basic needs. Erotic instinct and death instinct are the preeminent sources of motivation. A person's earlier life is dominated by the life instinct-the compulsion for self-preservation. Human beings experience sex urges and get sex gratification from the day of birth. He also felt that besides Erotic and Death instincts, "the unconscious" also plays an important role in one's behavior. A very high percent of a person's 'unconscious' remains below the surface and is therefore inaccessible. Unfilled needs, desires, wants, wishes, ideas or feelings form part of the 'unconscious.' Individual behavior patterns are dictated by this most powerful "unconscious."

4. Behaviorists' Learning Theory of Motivation says that if an individual behaves in a particular manner it is because of previous acts of learning and training received. Classical theory or operant conditioning theories support reinforcement. Albert Bandura felt that human motivation is directed through social rewards like praise.

5. Adler's Social Urges Theory felt that human motivation results primarily through social urges. He vehemently opposed Freud's advocating the sex motive as basis for motivation. Power, status, achievement, will-to-dominate and excel ensure a margin of safety and security. Security drive, therefore, is the basis for the motivation of human behavior.

6. Goal-oriented Theory of Cognitivism: argues that human motivation is guided by cognitive factors. Every behavior is goal-driven and therefore purposeful. The cognitive theory of motivation was propounded by William James, who felt that motivation is necessary to establish a psychomotor gap between ideas and actions. Leon Festinger's cognitive resonance theory points out that when two individual perceptions that are relevant to each other differ, dissonance is created. This creates confusion and tension, which is psychologically uncom-

fortable, and the concerned person will try to modify one of the incompatible perceptions with a view to reduce tension or dissonance. He tries his best to regain the original condition of consonance.

7. <u>Maslow's Self-Actualization Theory</u>: propounded by Abraham Maslow –"Motivation and Personality," tells us that there are many needs arranged in "hierarchies of prepotency." All these needs are closely knit and one need normally appears after the satisfaction of others.

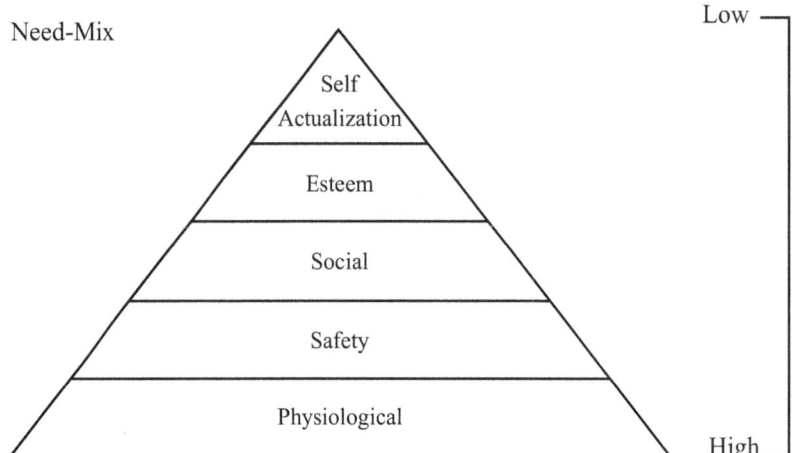

When physiological need is high:

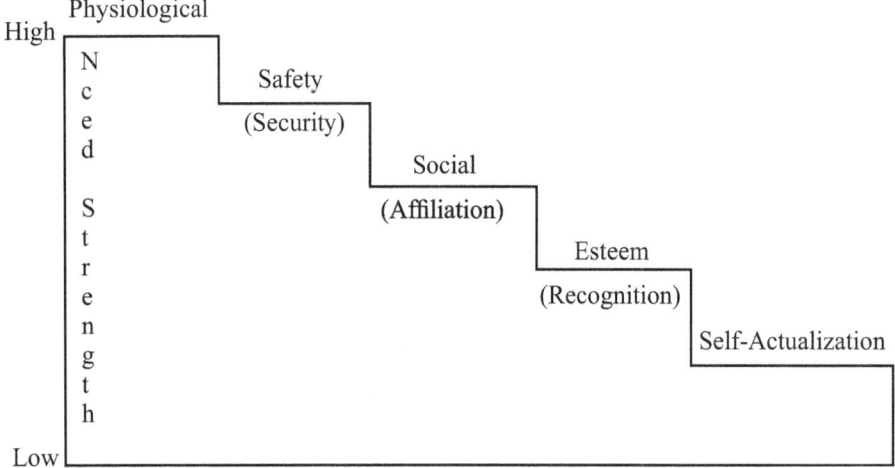

Once the physiological needs are satisfied then the need for safety (security) becomes pre-dominant.

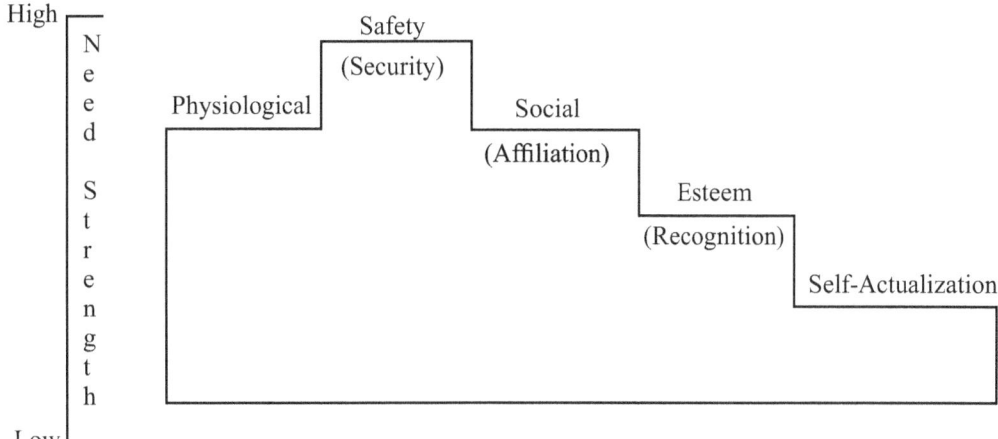

Likewise every need in the hierarchy become prominent after the previous need is satisfied. Let us see the self-actualization need:

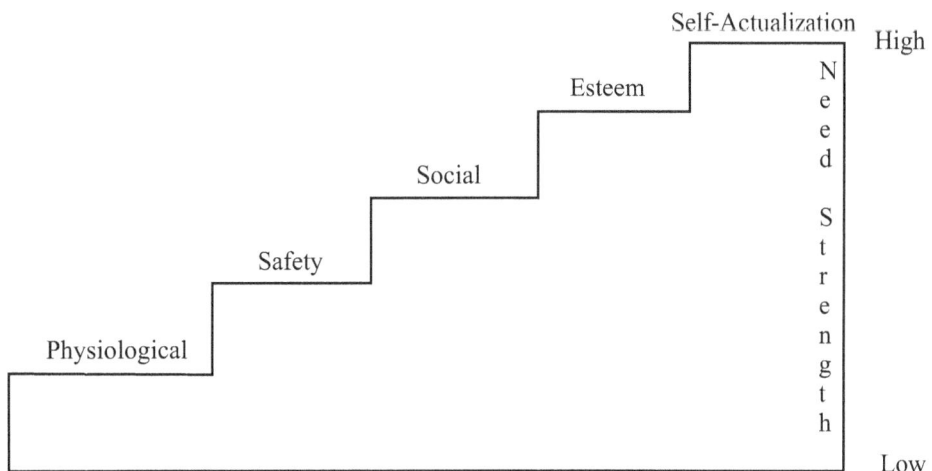

One's physiological need (say thirst) is satisfied, then the safety needs, after which social, then esteem come and finally the self-actualization need takes over. According to Maslow, self-actualization is "…what a man can be, he must be…" The self-actualization is the need, or want or desire to become what one is capable of becoming.

Individual Differences

F1: APTITUDE/ACHIEVEMENT

What is aptitude? According to Freeman, an erudite scholar: "…An aptitude is a combination of characteristics indicative of an individual's capacity to acquire some specific knowledge, skill, or set of organized responses, such as the ability to speak a language, to become a musician, to do mechanical work…" from the above definition you may notice that the nature of aptitude is mostly predictive. Example: Suppose you notice John playing tennis with his friends in the garden. When you say John has an aptitude for tennis, it means that he has the potential latent in him that his present condition or ability reveals that if proper training is imparted, he would be a successful player of tennis.

Many personality traits are products of both heredity and environment. Aptitude, a personality trait, naturally, has to be a product of both heredity and environment. "Aptitude" is predictive in nature. That is, it predicts the future success on the basis of the present condition. "Ability" restricts itself to the present performance of a given individual. "Achievement" indicates what a given individual has learned or acquired – "achievement" has past-orientation. "Aptitude" and "interest" are not synonyms. I may love playing tennis, i.e., I have tremendous interest in playing tennis; unfortunately I may not have "aptitude" for tennis. If you want to be a most successful player of tennis, you should have both interest and aptitude. "Intelligence" tests tell us what the general mental ability of a given individual is at a particular point in time. "Aptitude" tests tell us specific abilities of an individual. Musical aptitude tests like the "Seashore measure of musical talent" try to find musical talent in the candidate. Likewise, Clerical aptitude tests are meant to unearth talent for clerical work. Mechanical aptitude tests seek to establish a candidate's aptitude for mechanical work. Tests like "Meier-art-judgment test," seek to pinpoint in an individual aptitude for graphic art. There are specific tests for professional or scholastic skills. There are a number of standardized tests as well to unearth skills to suit various professions in the medical, para-medical, management, engineering, law, teaching and other fields. The range of application of aptitude tests is very wide indeed! They are very useful in predicating the suitability or otherwise of candidates meant for specific jobs!

F2: CREATIVITY

What is creativity? Let us now study some of the definitions given by learned people: According to Stagner and Karwoski as quoted by L.D. Crow and A. Crow in "Educational Psychology": "… Creativity implies the production of a totally or partially novel identity…" According to Levin M.J. (Psychology: A Biographical Approach.) (McGraw-Hill, 1978, p.311): "…Creativity is the ability to discover new solutions to problems or to produce new ideas, inventions or works of art. It is a special form of thinking, a way of viewing the world and interacting with it in a manner different from that of the general population…"

Creativity can be considered as a unique and novel personal experience. Some of the characteristics of creativity are:

1. Creativity is universal i.e. it is not restricted to any individual, group, caste, color or creed. There is no barrier, no age restriction, no location advantage nor any culture distinctiveness.

2. It is both an inborn and inherited trait as well as acquired skill. It is a gift of God and natural endowment combined. Education, training, experience, cultural backdrop, all these contribute towards nurturing creative expression.

3. Creativity is something different from the ordinary, something unique, something new and novel. Repetition or reproduction cannot be considered creativity.

4. Creativity means open thinking. Any creator should have freedom of thought and expression.

5. Creativity also depicts the ego of the creator. A certain amount of egoistic involvement of the creator is there in the expressions.

6. Creativity and anxiety are complementary. A creator's anxiety is different from a neurotic's. A creator's quest for excellence is his anxiety!

THEORIES OF CREATIVITY:

There are as eight theories: (1) God Given Gift Theory (a.k.a. Divine Inspiration Theory): Creativity is God given. A person can only be creative to the extent to which he has been blessed with divine power. (2) Insanity Theory: creativity and insanity go hand-in-hand. Both a creator and an insane person live in his own world. Cesare Lambroso believed in this theory. (3) Creativity is an inborn or native quality: This theory postulates that creativity is an inborn trait and with proper training an individual can be a successful creator. (4) Environmentally Gains Theory: According to this theory, creativity is not only God's blessing, or an inborn trait, but also shaped and sharpened by a positive environment. (5) Taylor's Level Theory: creativity, according to I.A. Taylor, exists at five levels in an ascending hierarchy. An individual can be considered creative only to the extent he is able he reach these levels. The five levels are: (a) Expressive creativity (spontaneous expression) (b) Productive creativity (innovative) (c) Inventive creativity (ingenuity and novel) (d) Innovative creativity (new ideas and/or principles), and, (e) Emergency creativity: (exceptional conceptualization of abstract assumption based on the premise of art or science. This level is very rare). (6) Hemisphere Theory: Creativity is the result of interaction between the Right and Left hemisphere of the brain. Creativity – right brain, logical and rational thinking – left brain. (7) Psycho-analytical Theory: Sigmund Freud belonged to one school of this theory. The vent of repressed desires, mostly sexual in nature, expresses in creativity. Another school led by C.G. Jung felt that the collective conscious was the cause for creativity. (8) Arielis Theory: According to the Arielis theory, the creativity process is the synthesis of (a) the primary process (unconscious, irrational thinking), and (b) the secondary process (developed mind, conscious level, rational thinking).

There are various stages in a creative process of which the following are important: (1) Preparation (2) incubation (3) illumination and (4) verification.
There are standardized verbal as well as non-verbal creativity-tests. (a) The Minnesota test of creative thinking, (b) Baqer Mehdi's tests of creativity thinking and (c) the Torrence tests of creative thinking are some of the standardized tests of creativity.

F3: CULTURAL INFLUENCES

The general beliefs, values, behavior, norms, language, even material articles that are passed from generation to generation are the hallmarks of any particular culture. We can safely say that culture is the lens through which we perceive, grasp and assess the society in which we live. We can also say that culture shows a child the ways of coping with the society around it as well as the world at large, as a result of each generation passing on its values, etc., to the next. Culture along with good social and educational opportunities in an open and nurturing environment plays a vital role in influencing the growth of a child in a positive way. Language is a very significant factor in any given culture. It enables a child to think coherently. Language teaches a child to be goal-directed as well as cooperative. It enables a child to share its experiences or thinking or ideas with others. A benchmark for desirable or undesirable behavior is the value system of a given culture. Norms are the rules and regulations that a culture imposes on its subjects with a view to obtain good behavior.

<u>Material-culture</u> Comprises of objects such as buildings, clothes, tools, arts, etc. <u>Non-material culture</u> (a.k.a. symbolic culture) comprises of a given group's thinking and behavioral patterns. <u>Ideal-culture</u> comprises of a given group's objectives, values and norms. <u>Real-culture</u> showcases a group's individual members' actual behavior, which may, (or, in most cases) may not conform to their ideal culture. <u>Ethnocentrism</u> is nothing but the way in which members of a given culture judge others. Invariably they use the group's culture as a benchmark, or measure in judging others. <u>Cultural relativism</u> on the other hand, tries to comprehend other cultures as they are; <u>Sub-culture</u> is a group within a given culture whose identity lights up its values and related behaviors in a distinguished way. The United States of America is a <u>Pluralistic society</u> comprising of innumerable groups, each having a set of its own values that distinguish it from the members of other groups within the broader culture!

F4: EXCEPTIONALITIES IN LEARNING: GIFTEDNESS, PHYSICAL HANDICAPS, BEHAVIOR DISORDERS

Exceptionalities, in this context, mean rare or unusual. Any individual who possesses traits that are considered to exhibit significant deviation from the normal or natural norms, is an exceptional or gifted individual. According to Telford and Sawrey (C.W. Telford and J.M. Sawrey, "The Exceptional Individual" – Prentice Hall, 1977. pp. 10 to 11) "…The term exceptional children refers to those children who deviate from the normal in physical, mental, emotional, or social characteristics to such a degree that they require special social and educational services to develop their maximum capacity…"

Gifted children can be defined as: "…The gifted are these who possess outstanding abilities or potential in the area of general intellectual capacity, specific academic aptitude, creative or productive thinking, leadership ability, visual or performing arts and psycho-motor activity…" [S. Marland, Education of the Gifted and Talented, Report of the Sub-committee on Education, Committee on Labor and Public Welfare, Washington D.C; U.S. Senate, 1972]

Gifted children exhibit above average intellectual growth and development. To identify and nurture such giftedness is the duty of any given society or its government. Such basic needs as security, love and a sense of belonging are to be provided. The basis of identification of a Gifted Child:

1. He/She learns very fast with relative ease.
2. Exhibits a crystal clear thinking capacity.
3. High retention rate of what is learned.
4. Has a large vocabulary.
5. Relies on practical knowledge and common sense.
6. Ability to perform tough mental tasks with relative ease.
7. Versatile – shows interest in a rather wide range of topics.
8. Very creative and exhibits originality in thinking.
9. Quicksilver reflexes, very observant and always on toes.

Gifted children are assets of a given nation. They should be encouraged by: (a) Providing separate schools (b) Separate classes (c) Double promotion and (d) other enrichment programs.

THE MENTALLY RETARDED:

What is mental retardation? It is a combination of the following:

(a) It is a state of mind

(b) Subnormal development and functioning of the brain or mind

(c) It is not a disease, and

(d) Observed at birth and further manifested during the cause of development.

The mentally retarded can be identified:

(1) Through lowly scores on standardized intelligent tests.

(2) Easily observable behavior of diminished intellectual functioning during the period of development.

(3) Deficient and defective adaptive behavior.

The best explanation of Mental Retardation came from the American Association on Mental Deficiency, 1983: "…Mental Retardation refers to significantly sub-average general intellectual functioning existing concurrently with deficits in adaptive behavior, and manifested during the development period…" The development period means the actual time period between conception and adolescence (normally 18th birthday).

Levels of Mental Retardation: (1) Mild (2) Moderate (3) Severe, and, (4) Profound. Mild ones can be educated, moderate ones can be trained but severe and profound ones can never be educated or trained. They have to be dependent on others. Backward children: According to Barton, Hall (Psychiatric Examination of the School Child, London): "…Backwardness in general, is applied to cases where their educational attainment falls below the level of their natural abilities…" Juvenile Delinquency: These are exceptional children with marked deviation in terms of social adjustment. They are called socially deviant. They possess tendencies that are considered criminal.

The Individuals with Disabilities Education Act (abbreviated IDEA) is a federal law which governs how states must provide special education and other services to students with disabilities. The law describes that the ultimate goal of special education is that the student will be prepared for continued education and independent living. The act applies to students from preschool age to 21 years old.

BEHAVIOR DISORDERS:

Behavior disorders do affect the academic life of a child. They are normally not connected to health factors nor are they reflected in intellect.

Generalized anxiety disorders (a.k.a. Anxiety neurosis) may be free-floating or all pervasive. The child is tense, worried and always feels inadequate. Such children cannot concentrate on studies or, even sports, cannot make decisions and most are oversensitive.

Obsessive compulsive disorders (OCD): in phobias, anxiety is caused mostly by external situations. However, in OCD anxiety is caused by internal situations such as persistent wishes or thoughts that intrude into a child's consciousness and therefore cannot be stopped. It includes either compulsions or obsessions that guide the child's behavior

Mutism: A child's inability to speak. In selective mutism the child, though able to speak very well in a particular setting, is unable to do so in certain other settings. The same child may be fluent at home with parents and other siblings, but may find it difficult to open up in the class.

Social phobias: A phobia is when a child (or patient) experiences panic attacks in a particular situation. A social phobia is characterized by a persistent fear in the individual to perform in an unfamiliar setting as the person inherently feels that he may be humiliated or embarrassed.

Dissociation (a.k.a. Separation Anxiety Disorders-SAD): it is an abnormal mental process in which any unpalatable fact is isolated by refusing recognition and thereby removed from memory. This involves the actual splitting off from consciousness of all unpalatable ideas so much so the patient is no longer aware of them.

Since behavior disorders can interfere with a child's family, school and even social situation, care should be taken by parents and teachers alike to provide a congenial, positive environment and the child should be encouraged to do better.

F5: INTELLIGENCE

According to Jean Piaget (The origins of intelligence in children): "…intelligence is the ability to adapt to one's surroundings…"

There are many intelligence tests to measure a child's intelligence. Mental Age signifies comparison with a particular mental level which is found to be generally normal for that age group. All human beings are not equal intelligence-wise; some are bright, some dull, but the vast majority are average! Even identical twins are not endowed with similar intelligence. There are intelligence tests that may classify as follows: (1) Individual Tests and, (2) Group Tests. There are verbal (language) tests as well as nonverbal (non-language tests).

Verbal tests consist of:

- Vocabulary tests
- Memory tests

- Comprehension Tests
- Information Tests
- Reasoning Tests
- Association Tests

Non-verbal Tests consists of:

- Army beta test
- Chicago non-verbal test
- Raven's progressive matrices test
- C.I.E non-verbal group tests, etc.

F6: NATURE VS. NURTURE

Nature: Individuals differ in many ways. There are (1) Physical differences (color, height, weight, hair, eye, etc.) (2) Mental differences (imagination, logic, concentration, creative ability) (3) Motor skills (4) Emotional differences (Positive vs. negative emotion) (5) Aptitude differences (6) Learning differences, etc. What decides these individual differences? (a) Heredity: According to Douglas O.B. and Holland B.F (Fundamentals of Educational Psychology): "…heredity consists of all the structure, physical characteristics, function or capacities derived from parents, other ancestry or species… " A fertilized ovum (zygote) comprises of cytoplasm (semi-fluid mass), which contains a nucleus, filled with chromosomes. Chromosomes exist in pairs.

In every cell of a chromosome, there are about 1,000 'genes' stored. The composition of 'genes' is determined by "DNA" and 'RNA.' DNA Deoxyribonucleic acid and RNA Ribonucleic acid. DNA is responsible for genetic inheritance, RNA acts as a helper to DNA in carrying out genetically coded information, or, messages from parent to child. Thus Nature plays a significant part in the individual differences seen in children.

Nurture: we know that the chromosomes with genes are transmitted to the offspring at the time of conception and here the role of heredity actually comes to an end. During the development of a fetus to a child inside the mother's womb, everything depends on the internal environmental influences of the mother. There is an impact on the development of a child from what the mother eats and drinks. The mother has to be happy and contented during pregnancy in order to avoid adverse effects on the baby's development. Therefore, it is necessary for the mother to be physically and mentally healthy during pregnancy. After a baby is born, the external environment takes over. Physical, cultural, sociological, as well as psychological factors of the environment influence and affect every aspect of the growth and development of a child. A child should be given a positive environment where he/she can grow without any hindrance. Proper care, good food, good education, instilling moral values, etc., will go a long way in the growth and development of a child.

F7: READING ABILITY

Reading ability comes under learning ability. It is now agreed that genetic factors play a very significant role in determining whether you possess Reading ability or disability. Two distinct reading problems have been linked to chromosome-6 (phonologic awareness) and chromosome-15 (single-ward reading) – [Breitchman and Yound] In the United States nearly 4% of school-going children suffer from Reading Disability.

Today, communication both oral and written plays a significant role in the success of an individual both in the commercial as well as in the personal sphere. Every type of information is available in the printed form, in more than a billion web pages browsed online.

There are two major aspects to successful reading: comprehension and decoding. Reading comprehension is the ability to understand what a series of words means. The goal of reading instruction is to ensure that students are able to grow in their comprehension of the things that they are reading, and to be self-sufficient in their future efforts. One of the common problems that student's face with reading comprehension is if they are unsuccessful at the second aspect, decoding.

Decoding refers to the ability to mentally group letters into recognizable groups to help increase reading speed and understanding. In the basic sense, decoding is word recognition. As students learn to better recognize familiar and recurring letter groupings as words, then they will be able to expend less effort in recognizing the word, and focus more attention on understanding what they are reading. Helping students to become more familiar with letters and sounds, and using repetition of common sounds and words will help to increase decoding abilities.

Testing

G1: ASSESSMENT OF INSTRUCTIONAL OBJECTIVES; BIAS IN TESTING; CLASSROOM ASSESSMENT

Children at different developmental stages are to be taught and therefore the instructional objectives should be very carefully thought out and executed. Care should be taken to ensure that the educational Philosophy of the institution dove-tails with the overall governmental policy on education. One should assess one's instructional objectives constantly and modify the material content in accordance with the changing needs. (1) Learning experiences should be in line with the developmental stages of children (2) A grade-wise curriculum should be made available. (3) One should assess the individual differences as well as individuality of the children taught and the syllabi should reflect this important fact. (4) One should constantly assess whether the learning experiences imparted to children reflect their age, grade, individual potentialities, skills, etc.

Always there should be valid answers for the following questions when assessing the instructional objectives: (1) WHO is being taught, (2) WHAT is being taught, and, (3) What is the OBJECTIVE in such teaching? A child grows constantly and his mental faculties do develop accordingly day by day. Also ensure whether the instructional objectives are being conveyed with appropriate, proper and effective communication so that the learning experiences reach the students without any hiccup. What sort of learning assistance an individual child needs should be constantly assessed so that the child gets all the help he needs at the RIGHT TIME.

Bias in Testing: A Test tries to evaluate a child's learning experiences to find out whether he has learned the learning objectives or is still in the process of learning. Tests are designed to assess a child's present learning conditions in the areas of (a) Verbal information (b) Motor skills (c) Cognitive skills (d) Intellectual skills and (e) Attitudes. Most of the tests are designed to bring out the academic progress of a child. Such academic achievements can only be the raw material and not the end-products in human development. Tests only signify a particular child's academic progress in a given classroom on the subjects meticulously taught. How about the vast array of nonacademic subjects?

Tests cannot tell the exact state of affairs of a child's learning experience in such diverse objectives.

Classroom Assessment: Classroom assessment is very important as it tells the teacher where each student is in regard to individual subjects taught. The teacher will be able to highlight the student's strengths and weaknesses and determine where corrective measures are needed. The teacher can also apprise the parents of the progress his ward has made in the class. Nowadays custom-made tests are set for children, which allow a detailed, a specific and a totally individualized evaluation. In a classroom assessment, a teacher, if he wants to know the writing skills of students, has no choice but to go in for an "Essay" type test. If he wants to know whether the students remember what was taught, he would opt for either a "Multiple choice" test or "True-or-false" test, or "Matching-Test." "Essay Tests," once very popular among teachers, are increasingly shunned.

G2: DESCRIPTIVE STATISTICS; NORM AND CRITERION-REFERENCED TESTS; SCALES SCORE/STANDARD DEVIATION

Statistics can be bifurcated into (1) Descriptive statistics and (2) Inferential statistics. Descriptive statistics supply you with data and tell you what it is all about. In inferential statistics, you not only have data but try to go beyond the data by resorting to a conclusion based on the data.

Descriptive statistics prepare and present quantitative data in a meaningful way. A vast chunk of information is reduced into a small lot of verifiable data in Descriptive Statistics. The case in point is Grade Point Average-GPA, where a solitary unit seeks to illustrate any given student's performance across a wide array of learning experiences. You cannot infer or conclude anything from such descriptive statistical data. It is also possible to have distortions if the approach is not methodical. At best descriptive statistics can be used to compare one unit with another from the small summary of data given.

Norm-referenced and criterion-referenced tests are mostly misunderstood because of an inability to distinguish the basic differences between the two.

When it comes to understanding test scores, there are a number of values which can be taken into consideration. Mean, median, mode and range are some important terms in analyzing and understanding data as a set. The mean of a set of data is also called (more commonly but less correctly) the average, because it is one method of determining the average or "normal" value for a set of data. To find the mean, add all of the numbers in a data set and divide the total by the total number of data points. For example the mean of 3, 4, 5, and 6 is 3+4+5+6 which equals 28 divided by 4 because there are four numbers. 28/4= 4.5. Therefore the mean is 4.5.

The median is the middle number in a set of data when it is organized from highest to lowest. This is another way of finding the "normal" value in a set of data. For example, the median of the data set 3, 3, 4, 5, 6, 7, 8 would be 5. The main different between the median and the mean is that the mean is more influenced by one extreme value. For example, if most of the scores are in the eighties range, but one student got a twenty percent, the median will remain fairly similar whereas the mean may be pulled down more significantly.

The mode, a third way of finding the "normal" value in a set of numbers, is the value that occurs most commonly. For example, the mode of 3, 3, 4, 5, 5, 5, 8, 9 would be 5 because it appears three times. The mode is less commonly used than mean or median.

The range of a set of data is the difference between the highest and lowest values. For example, the range of the set 2, 2, 3, 4, 8, 9, 15, 21 would be 21-2 or 19. The range can be important in analyzing test scores because it can show how closely grouped the scores were. If the test had a high mean, for example 91 percent, but it also has a high range, such as 80, it would indicate that most of the class understood but a few of them are really struggling. On the other hand, if the mean were 91 and the range were 10 it would indicate that all of the students in the class understood the concept.

Another way to look at test scores is through percentiles. These values are used to analyze data points as they compare to the whole set. It is important to remember that a percentile is different from a percentage. A percentage determines the fraction (over of the questions that are correct. A percentile describes the number of scores at or below any chosen score. For example, if a percentage of 85 is in the 90th percentile, this means that 90 percent of the scores were less than 85.

Percentiles are found using z scores. Z scores are also called standard scores. This is because z scores are used to analyze data, not in terms of numerical value, but in terms of distance from the mean. The units of z scores are standard deviations. This means that a z score of 1 would describe a value which is one standard deviation, or σ, away from the mean. Standard deviation is essentially a description of how far away, on average, the values in a data set are from a mean. Standard deviation can be found using a graphing calculator. Z scores are calculated using the formula $z = (x-\mu)/\sigma$, where x is the value being studied, μ is the mean of the data set and σ is the standard deviation. The percentile can be found using either a table of standard values or graphing calculator.

One way of using percentiles is in grading by a bell curve. The easiest way to understand what a bell curve is is to think of a histogram. A histogram is like a bar graph, but the variables are both numbers. Across the x axis is the score, and the y axis is the number of times that value appears (the number of people that got that score). If you were to draw a line around the histogram, and it were shaped approximately like a bell, it would be called a bell curve (not every curve does this). For example:

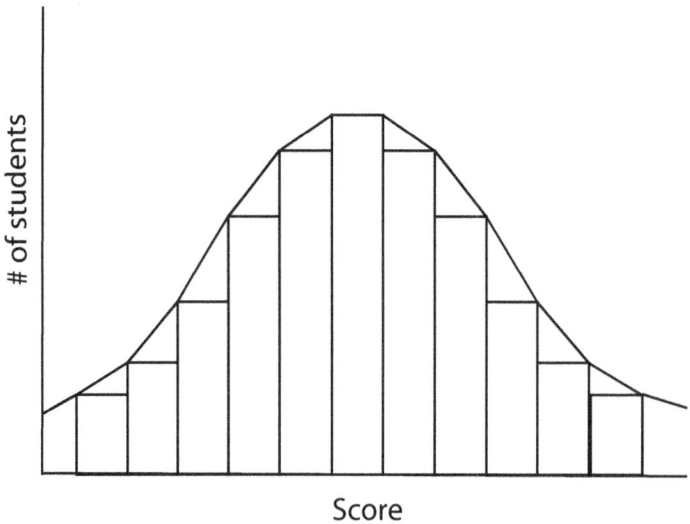

Essentially, each section of the bell curve can be broken down into percentiles and z scores. The highest point on the curve will be both the median and mean, making the values to the right "above average" and the values to the left "below average." The curve can be broken down into sections so that based on what percentile the score is in, the student will receive the corresponding grade. For example:

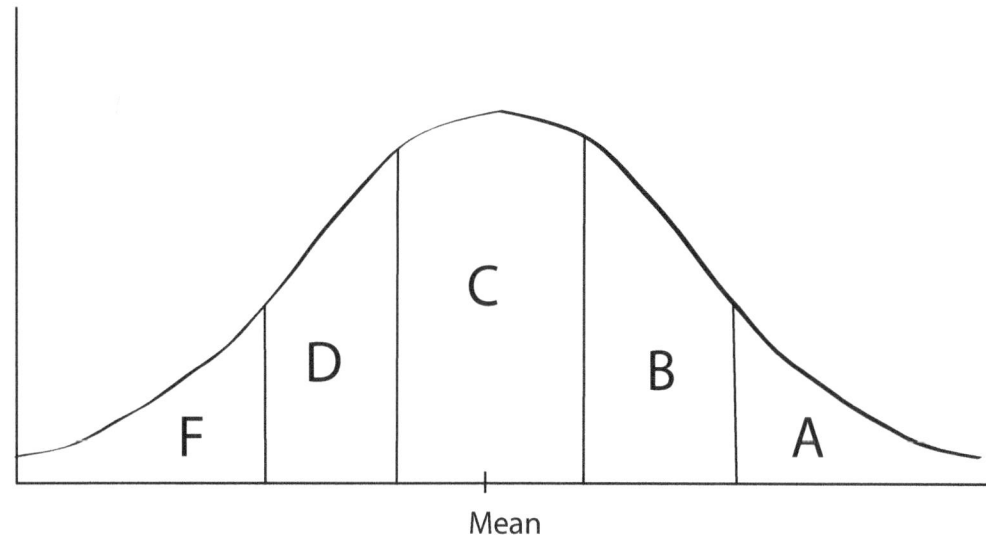

The 'X' axis represents one variable and the "Y" axis represents another. "Scales" are arranged vertically and horizontally representing the "Y" and "X" axis respectively. Normally "Scales" should be placed at the left and at the bottom of the graph; sometimes the vertical scale as well as horizontal scale.

An important rule in statistics is the 68-95-99 Rule. This rule is used in analyzing normally distributed data sets. When a set of data is described as "normal" it means that it creates a perfect bell curve around the mean value of the set. The standard deviation of a data set is the average distance of a particular point from that mean (the center point of the data). According to the 68-95-99 rule, 68% of the data falls within one standard deviation of the mean in either direction, 95% percent within two standard deviations, and 99% within three standard deviations. This information can be useful in determining percentiles and other important aspects about the data.

G3: TEST CONSTRUCTION; TEST RELIABILITY; TEST VALIDITY; USE AND MISUSE OF ASSESSMENT TECHNIQUES

A class teacher knows what he has taught. He would therefore like to know whether his students understood what he taught. Standard tests are resorted to by schools and the instructional methods and materials are clearly prescribed. It is normal practice in schools for the class teacher to construct his tests on the following basis: (1) If he wants to know the students' memory and recall, he may construct a "True-False"-loaded test paper. (2) If he wants to find out the discriminative judgment of his students, he would construct a "Multiple-choice"-loaded test paper (3) If he wants to know whether his students understand certain relationships between given pieces of information, he may construct a "Matching-Test"-loaded test paper. (4) If he wants to know the general expressive ability of a student, he will construct an "Essay-type" test paper. (5) Generally, nowadays teachers construct a test paper incorporating one, two, or all the above methods.

TEST RELIABILITY:

In the area of evaluation-practices "reliability" refers to the consistency shown by a student on the subjects tested over a period of time.

Test Validity: A teacher constructs a test to find out his students' comprehension of the subjects he assiduously taught. If such a test succeeds in its basic task, it is said to have validity.

Assessment techniques are used effectively by most teachers but there are some who misuse them for catering to their ego.

Pedagogy

The word "Pedagogy" is derived from two Greek roots – "paidos" = child, and "agogos" = leading. Pedagogy is, therefore, "the leading of children." Where does a teacher lead a child – of course, to learning, to development, to maturity!

H1: ADVANCE ORGANIZERS; BILINGUAL/ESL INSTRUCTION; CLARITY/ORGANIZATION

"Advance Organizers" was propounded by D. Ausubel. It seeks to study how children learn quite a good amount of appropriate material from data/text and verbal learning experiences gained in a school backdrop. The learning process is based on reception of information. How to co-relate the existing knowledge in the cognitive structure with that of the new material learned is the primary process in learning. According to Ausubel instructional effectiveness can be augmented by using the advance organizers. He states in his wonderful book: "The Psychology of Meaningful Verbal Learning":

"…These organizers are introduced in advance of learning itself, and are also presented at a higher level of abstraction, generality, and inclusiveness; and since the substantive content of a given organizer or series of organizers is selected on the basis of its suitability for explaining, integrating and interrelating the material they precede, this strategy simultaneously satisfies the substantive as well as the programming criteria for enhancing the organization strength of cognitive structure…"

All ethnic groups are mostly bilingual – they speak and write their own language like Chinese, or Italian, or German depending upon the ethnic group to which they belong, and also may speak and write the majority language – English. For such people ESL Instruction should be very carefully thought out and taught. As the U.S. is a country of immigrants from all over the world, ESL (English as a Second Language) has acquired significance. Care should be taken to teach the nuances including proper accent, which is very important. Grammar, sentence construction, speech delivery, spelling and importantly vocabulary building are to be seen as vital aspects in ESL instruction.

When it comes to bilingual education, the two basic types of approaches are transitional and maintenance. The transitional approach has its main focus of integrating the student in mainstream classes. Although some of the material is taught in their native language, most of it (around 70%) will be taught in the target language (generally English). Although the idea is to teach partially in the native language to keep the student up to speed with what they need to know for the class, this type of bilingual education is often associated with low test scores. The maintenance approach has a focus on enrichment of the student. It focuses on maintaining the student's primary language, while teaching them a second language as well. This is a more truly bilingual approach as it attempts to enhance a student's skills with both languages.

What is clarity? It means the quality of expressing ideas or thoughts in a clear way. There should be clarity of thought and clarity of action. There should be substance in content. Coherent, cogent expression is needed in good instruction. Organization refers to the act of planning and arranging things in a most effective manner. Organization is the backbone of any meaningful activity, including teaching. The instructions should have clarity of thought and ideas and the instructional material organized in a most systematic and methodical manner coupled with coherent, cogent expressions and good comprehension. Such classroom instructions will be met with success.

H2: CLASSROOM MANAGEMENT; COOPERATIVE LEARNING; DISCOVERY AND RECEPTION LEARNING

First a class teacher should see whether he has a homogenous age group of students or he has a group whose age difference wildly fluctuates. Normally in the United States, the average age difference in a class of 30 would be around one year. Suppose the age difference is 4 to 5 years, then there will be problems in teaching as well as learning.

Again a teacher has to segregate his class on the basis of his findings of his students' intelligence, viz., above average, average and below average, and group such students accordingly. Here he has to manage his classroom by imparting knowledge in such a way that it reaches each group.

He should thoroughly think about the subject material to be taught and decide how he is going to put it across for easy absorption. He can give lectures; he can use drawings and pictures. He can use visual media or he can also use computers.

The students should learn and be able to reproduce what they have learned in their own language. A teacher should manage his classroom enforcing discipline, without which no class will be able to advise results. A teacher's class management should also include a good progress evaluation technique from the results of which he should be able to know the strengths and weaknesses of his students. He should make the classroom a most congenial place where learning becomes easy.

Cooperative learning has its own merits. Competition is good as it is recognized as a lever of motivation of young children. In fact there were many experiments conducted on very young children and the results obtained suggested that the cooperative responses rather than competitive responses were more conspicuous in them. Pure competition through a known motivator yet suffers many shortcomings. Cooperative rivalry is the answer. Individuals belonging to a group are bound to cooperate with each other but compete with rival groups. Such cooperative learning develops team spirit and self discipline besides keeping the morale of the group high.

What is "Discovery" and "Reception Learning"? In discovery learning a student should be left to discover the information sought through problem solving. This is against 'rote' learning in which there won't be any meaningful material available as it won't be necessary. In reception learning a great amount of detailed material is available and that is why it is also known as "expository" learning.

A **token economy** is the term for a type of system that is set up based on the principle of rewards. The rewards are known as tokens. Particularly in elementary schools, token economies are considered a good form of motivation and reward. Essentially, whenever an individual does something noteworthy they are given a token that can be redeemed later. Tokens can be anything from coins, to tickets, to pieces of paper with marks on them. The important thing is that there is an established method to redeem the tokens. Beyond that, token economies take advantage of positive reinforcement to influence the behavior of participants.

Many different skills and abilities are involved with effective teaching. The ability to master and apply various techniques leads some teachers to be classified as experts while others remain novices. Novice teachers are often newer to the field of teaching. Although they may be enthusiastic and excited about the prospect of teaching, they have little experience and haven't mastered lesson planning or classroom management. Expert teachers typically have a much better grasp of curriculum and class interaction.

Whereas novice teachers tend to focus on meeting the specific curriculum and study requirements, expert teachers are able to teach a long-term view of the class and integrate the curriculum into the teaching pattern that they consider important. Because of the technical expertise of the teacher, students are able to become more involved, attentive, and interactive. Expert teachers also expand their understanding beyond just the curriculum of the class. They are able to see the individual needs of students, and structure the class so that all students can be successful. To become an expert teacher takes experience and dedication.

H3: INSTRUCTIONAL DESIGN AND TECHNIQUE; PSYCHOLOGY OF CONTENT AREAS; TEACHER EXPECTATION/PYGMALION EFFECT/WAIT-TIME

The first task of a teacher is to plan and organize the material to be taught. He should select the material from authentic sources. He should know his class and be able to teach according to the needs. There is no point in teaching "Calculus" to a high school student who is not ready. He should be clear in his mind that he will teach what is needed by the class, not more, not less. Will he only deliver lectures or include question and answer sessions in between? Are drawings and photographs to be shown as illustrations? Will he introduce for certain subjects the concept of "group dynamics"? Should he for certain subjects introduce audio visual aids as part of his instructional design? Today, there is a veritable information explosion. In such a scenario, it is not a good idea to introduce 'computer' and 'internet' for some subjects. The idea is to make the students understand what he teaches. Instructions should be designed accordingly.

Contents should be psychologically-backed materials like learning, memory, interpersonal skills, behavior and attitude, growth and development, individual differences, all have psychological theory backing them, which is to be reflected. Contents should be easy to understand and easy to recall.

If a class teacher expects a group of students in his class to do well, it invariably happens that such students do really well. This is the "Teacher Expectation" hypothesis. There were a few experiments conducted in classroom situations and the results proved that the students the teacher expects to do better, always do better. This is what is known as the "Pygmalion Effect" (the name taken from a drama by George Bernard Shaw). It proved that the expectation of a teacher is definitely one of the determinants in the performance of a student.

The Pygmalion Effect is an example of self-fulfilling prophecy. It was developed primarily by Robert Rosenthal and describes a phenomenon that when teacher's expectations of students are higher, the students will learn and achieve more as a direct result.

In one experiment, they studied a number of the classes in an elementary school (with classes covering each grade). In each class, the teachers were led to believe that a few randomly selected students (the experimental group) would soon be showing a burst of intellectual growth. All of the students took IQ tests at the beginning and end of the year. For the experiment, the average IQ rise for the control group students was around eight and the average raise for the experimental group was around twelve. However, in some cases the improvement was as large as twelve for the control group and twenty eight for the experimental group.

Dr. Mary Budd Rowe is famous for studying the concept of wait time in classrooms. Rowe's studies showed that after asking a question a teacher will typically wait an average of one second for a response. At that point they will expand the question, ask again, or break the silence in some other way. Rowe's studies showed that if instructors will simply increase that amount of time, called the "wait time," then it changes the whole tone of the classroom. By increasing the wait time to 3-5 seconds students will typically give longer, better-explained, and more thorough answers.

Research, Design and Analysis

I1: THE SCIENTIFIC METHOD; RESEARCH METHODS; READING CHARTS AND GRAPHS; EXPERIMENTS

To study the way that people grow, learn, adapt and interact with others, psychologists use a standardized method so that other people in the scientific community can understand their findings and agree on research.

Scientists use a specific vocabulary to conduct their research. A **participant** is a person that a scientist studies in their experiment. They can also be referred to as a subject. When a scientist is performing an experiment on an animal, they are also referred to as a subject or a participant.

When scientists want to study an entire city, culture, or population, they will use a sample. A **sample** is a small collection of subjects. The number of people you need to participate to make the sample the most accurate is statistically generated based on the amount of the population.

Everything that a scientist measures and studies is called a **variable**. For example, if you were conducting research on insomnia, you would have variables which include the amount of time it takes a person to fall asleep, how much caffeine they ingest, how much alcohol or drugs they ingest, what distractions are in the room, etc.

Research must meet four main tests:

1. Research must be **replicable**. Another scientist, given the information regarding the experiment, should be able to reproduce the experiment with the same results. This is how the scientific community accepts or rejects new theories. If the experiment can be reproduced several times by different people in different organizations or locations, it lends to its credibility. This means that the theory must be quantitative, or measurable and not qualitative. Qualitative means that something is similar in structure or organization but it cannot be measured in numerical terms.

2. The research must be **falsifiable**. This means that a theory has to be stated in a way that can be rejected or accepted. Think of it as asking a yes or no question. Is smoking bad for you? The answer is yes or no, and can be proven. This could be stated as "smoking is bad for you because it contains carcinogens". This is a falsifiable statement. It needs to be stated this way so that it can be proved or disproved. If a researcher does not consider all the evidence, but ignores the information that does not prove their theory and accepts the information that proves it, they are showing **confirmation bias**.

3. The research must be precisely stated and conducted. A theory needs to be stated precisely so it can be replicated. Scientists use operational definitions to state exactly how a variable will be measured. For example, a researcher studying birth order may notice that children who are the oldest of several siblings tend to be more responsible as adults and parents. The researcher may conclude that this is because they have experienced more time nurturing and caring for younger siblings. In our birth order study, the scientist needs to find a way to measure "responsible". He or she might decide that they will use the individual's credit reports as an operational variable to show responsibility.

4. Researchers must use the most logical, simplest explanation possible as an answer to their theory. This is also called the **principle of parsimony** or **Occam's razor**.

THE SCIENTIFIC METHOD

The Scientific Method is the accepted way to conduct research. It contains several steps. First, a researcher created a hypothesis. This is the testable idea. Second, information is gathered through an experiment or research. This information either proves or disproves the theory which leads to the third step, refining the theory. At this point, it may be necessary to start the experiment all over, having applied the new information learned in the experiment. The fourth and final stage is developing a theory. Again, at this point, it is necessary to test the theory through the scientific method. Once a theory has been proved successfully by reputable researchers, the more times it is reproduced, the more credibility it has.

RESEARCH METHODS

Information for a theory or experiment can be gathered several ways.

Case Study

In a case study, a single individual (subject) is intensely studied. The researcher gets data through personal interview with the subject, its employees, neighbors, contacts, etc., and by reviewing documentation or records (i.e., medical history, family life, etc.). Other sources for information are testing and direct observation of the subject.

Survey

A survey is a great way to get information about a specific type of information. For example, a survey would work well to measure performance in an office environment. These can be aggregated and used to improve employee performance. Usually with a survey, questionnaires are given out to participants who are then asked to answer questions to the best of their ability. When a participant fills out a survey themselves *about* themselves, it is called self-report data. This information can possibly not be as reliable as other research methods because subjects may be dishonest with their answers. For example, the question "Are you ever late to work?" may have respondents answering "no" when in fact, they are late but either do not remember that or are dishonest to avoid punishment or negative information about themselves. Many answer with the answers they feel that researchers (or themselves) want to hear instead of the truth.

Naturalistic Observation

Jean Piaget extensively used natural observation to study children. Naturalistic observation is when a researcher observes and studies subjects without interacting or interfering with them. Piaget observed the behavior of children playing in the schoolyard to access developmental stages. Another example well known to television viewers of the series "Star Trek" involves "The Prime Directive". This is the most perfect version demonstrated (in fiction) of naturalistic observation. In the show, the researchers had the ability to view and study human cultures without being known to the subjects because of their advancements in technology. In the series, it was a great violation to interact with and impact the development of these cultures and societies.

Laboratory Observation

Laboratory observation is conducted in a laboratory environment. This method is selected to monitor specific biological changes in individuals. In a lab setting, expensive and sophisticated machinery can be used to study the participants. Sometimes one-way mirrors are used to observe the participants.

Psychological Tests

Psychological tests give information about participants. Some of the more common include standardized tests such as the Minnesota Multiphasic Personality Inventory also known as the MMPI (a personality test), aptitudes, interests, etc. A participant's score is then compared to the norms for that test. A test is valid if it measures what it is supposed to. For example, a test on depression will be able to measure a person's depression. If it cannot, then the test is not valid. Content validity is applied when a test measures something with more that one facet. For example, a test for overall cooking skills would not be valid if it only tested baking cakes and not other skills such as grilling meat or making soup.

Cross Sectional Studies

When people of different ages are studied at one particular time it is called a cross sectional study, because you have a cross section of the population or demographic that you want to study.

Longitudinal Studies

Longitudinal studies are when people are followed and studied over a long period of time and check up on at certain points. These are best used to study the development of certain traits and track health issues. An example of a longitudinal study would be: 600 infants that were put up for adoption were tracked for several years. Some infants were adopted, some returned to the birth mothers and some were put into foster care. Which group adjusted the best and why?

Correlation Research

Correlation research is used to show links between events, people, actions, behaviors, etc. Correlation research does not determine the causes of behavior but is linked to statistics. Causation is the cause of something. Correlation is not causation. This is an example of FAULTY, incorrect causation: a child eats an ice cream three times a week. This child scores well on school aptitude tests. It is determined that eating ice cream will make you smarter and do better on tests. There are additional factors or many others including socioeconomic status resulting from educated parents who genetically pass on their aptitude for school as well as their influence on the importance of school. In this situation, it is most likely the parents who contribute to the child's aptitude scores.

When conducting a survey and you have completed compiling the data, you will be able to measure the correlation between certain traits and variables tested. A correlation coefficient measures the strength between the two variables. A correlation coefficient is a number between -1 and +1.

A positive correlation means that when one variable increases, the other variable increases as well. For example, the more a couple fights, the more likely they are to get a divorce.

When one variable increases and the other variable decreases it is called a negative correlation. An example of this would be babies that are held by their caregivers tend to cry less. When the amount of time they are held goes up, the time they cry goes down.

The higher the number of the correlation coefficient, the stronger the correlation. A +0.9 or -0.9 shows a very strong correlation because the number is closest to a whole positive number 1 or a whole negative number 1. A weak correlation is a +0.1 or a -0.1. A correlation of zero shows that there is no relationship between variables.

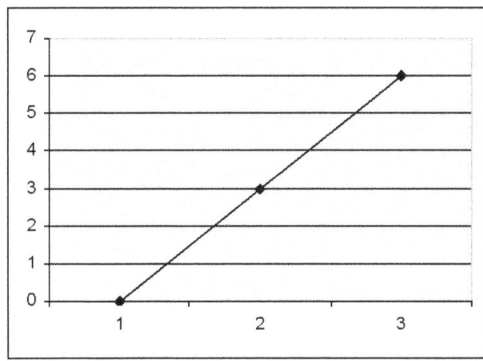
Positive correlation

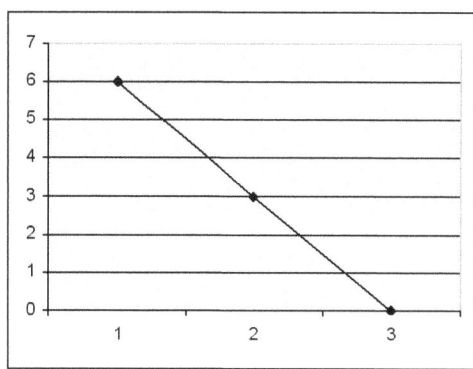
Negative correlation

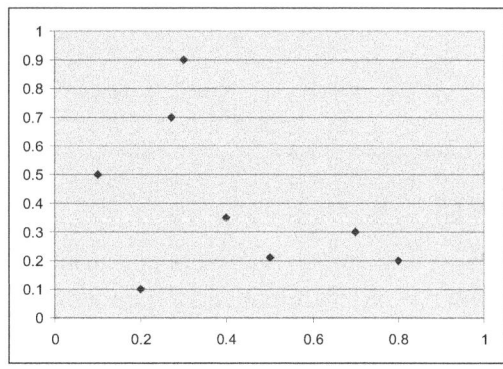
No correlation (above)

Census

A census is a collection of data from all cases or people in the chosen set. Usually, the most common form of a census would take place within an entire school of state. This means that every person of that school or state must be included. Censuses are usually not performed because they are so expensive. A census is valuable because it gives an accurate representation. To save time and money, survey companies will ask 1000 people or so (remember, the number changes based on the amount of people to be surveyed. A good rule of thumb is 10%). This is called sampling. For example, a recent census shows that the single person is the fastest-growing household type. So basically, a sample is a set of cases of people randomly chosen from a large group. The sample is to represent the group. The larger the sample, the more accurate the results.

READING CHARTS AND GRAPHS

Charts and graphs are easy ways to display information and make it easily readable.

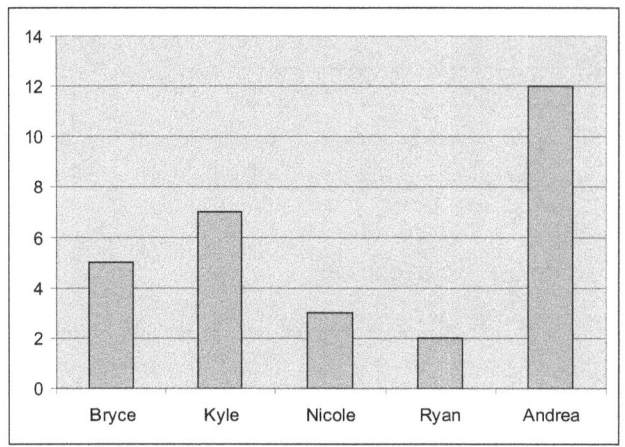

EXPERIMENTS

In experiments, a researcher manipulates variables to test theories and conclusions. Each experiment has independent and dependent variables. This is how researchers test cause and effect links and relationships.

The independent variable is the variable that researchers have direct control over. Dependent variable is then observed by the researcher.

In experiments, there are usually two groups of participants. One group is the experimental group and one group is the control group. The most common example is in medical trials. Let's say there is a trial run of a new diet drug. The researcher will split the group randomly in two. Group 1 will receive the diet pill that is being tested. Group 2 will receive a placebo pill. The placebo pill is simply a sugar pill. Group 2 will not know that they are not receiving the real drug. This allows the researchers to study the true effectiveness and side-effects of the pill. When the people are assigned to a group randomly, it is called **random assignment**. This particular experiment was a single-blind experiment. A **double-blind** experiment is when none of the doctors, researches and participants know who is getting the real drug. It is assigned by computer or an independent individual where it is kept confidential until the conclusion of the study.

When a participant starts to feel the effects of the drug but is *actually* taking a sugar pill or placebo it is called the **placebo effect**.

It is very important to avoid bias in research. Bias is the distortion of the results. Common types of bias include the sampling bias, subject bias and researcher bias. The placebo effect is an example of subject bias. Experimenter or researcher bias is avoided by conducting a double-blind experiment.

There are some disadvantages to experiments. They cannot be used to study everything. There are officially defined rules how humans and animals must be treated with the experiment. In an infamous experiment by psychologist Stanley Milgram, subjects were told that they were giving painful electric shocks to other people when in reality they were not. Some people consider this experiment unethical because it caused the participants emotional discomfort.

Researchers must get consent from their participants before conducting experiment. Informed consent means that the participants must know the content of the experiment and be warned of any risk or harm.

12: RESEARCH ANALYSIS AND STATISTICS

Research and analysis are part and parcel of educational psychology. Educational psychologists have worked relentlessly to analyze data on many aspects of the subjects in order to arrive at meaningful generalizations, principles and theories. Measuring intelligence has facilitated teachers to know how well a given child can do through the learning experience provided by him. Binet's (a French psychologist) contribution towards assessment of children on a 'scale of average,' above average and below average helped teaching to a great extent.

In the areas of "transfer of learning," "retro-active inhibition" and "forgetting," E.J. Swenson has contributed immensely through his tireless research and analysis.. ["Organization and Generalization as Factors in Learning, Transfer and Retro-active inhibition in Learning Theory in School Situations"]

In the area of "behavior" and "behavior modifications" there have been significant contributions from a number of educationalists and psychologists from Elton May to Freud to Thorndike and many more. Still research and analysis continue.

Statistics is a very important aspect of data presentation in a methodical and systematic way. Educational psychology needs (1) organized data for presentation purposes (2) group performance measurements (3) individual performance movements (4) to assess relationships, and (5) on the basis of analysis, come to conclusions.

 Government In Education

J1: IDEA

The most current federal law dealing with the process for ensuring special education where it is needed is the Individuals with Disabilities Education Act, also known as IDEA. The act identifies thirteen different areas of coverage for which special education services must be provided for by the school at no cost to the parents. These are autism, deaf-blindness, deafness, emotional disturbance, hearing impairment, intellectual disability, multiple disabilities, orthopedic impairment, other health impairment (including ADHD), specific learning disabilities (such as dyslexia), speech or language impairment, traumatic brain injury, and visual impairment. When the school suspects that a student may be suffering from one or more disabilities then they are expected to test the child to verify, and to determine their specific needs. Based on the law there are two things that qualify a student for special education. Firstly, they must be confirmed to have a disability, and secondly that disability must be impairing their ability to perform well in school.

Once it is determined that a child does require and qualify for special education, then the school and parents work together to develop and Individual Education Plan (IEP). An IEP is a legal document that specifies the responsibilities of the school in helping a child to receive the best education possible. It may specify specific exceptions that will be made for the student, whether they should attend certain classes, or any other services the school will provide. The IEP will also outline goals for the student, and how those goals will be measured and evaluated. It's important that parents know that they have an important say in each phase of their child's education. They should work with the school in developing the IEP and in further monitoring to help their child achieve educational success.

J2: PUBLIC LAW 94-142

Public Law 94-142, also known as the Education of All Handicapped Children Law, was the first law to ensure that children with special needs would receive an education. It was essentially the precursor to what is now known as the Individuals with Disabilities Education Act. The name was changed when the law was updated in 1990.

The goals of P.L. 94-142 were to ensure that all students that needed special education would receive it, to ensure that the services would be fair and accessible, and to help provide federal funds for such programs. The law required that any school that accepted federal funds must provide special education where needed, and in a way that was a close to the mainstream learning process as possible.

 Sample Test Questions

An important note about these test questions. Read before you begin. Our sample test questions are NOT designed to test your knowledge to assess if you are ready to take the test. While all questions WILL test your knowledge, some or all may cover new areas that are not previously covered in this study guide. This is intentional. For questions that you do not answer correctly, take the time to study the question and the answer to prepare yourself for the test.

1) Educational psychology is a course about

   A) Politics dealing with education
   B) Development of a child
   C) The art of teaching
   D) The science of psychology
   E) None of the above

The correct answer is C:) The art of teaching. Educational psychology is a course about the science and art of teaching.

2) A parent notices that their children never do their homework, and instead spend all of their time playing on the computer. How could they apply the Premack principle?

   A) By allowing their children to do their homework after they have gotten B) bored with the computer.
   B) By grounding their children from the computer so that they are then forced to do their homework.
   C) By accepting that their children do not enjoy homework and allowing them to play quite often.
   D) By not allowing their children to play on the computer until their homework has been completed.
   E) By punishing their children with increasing severity each time their homework is not completed.

The correct answer is D:) By not allowing their children to play on the computer until their homework has been completed. The Premack principle uses a desired activity, such as the computer, as a reinforcer to make a less desired activity, such as homework, more probable.

3) The definition of Psychology is

    A) The study of teaching
    B) The study of development
    C) The study of human behavior and experience
    D) The study of childhood
    E) The study of the family

The correct answer is C:) The study of human behavior and experience. Human behavior and experience are what define us as individuals.

4) What is the median of the following data set?

    1, 2, 6, 9, 12, 15, 17, 18, 21, 15, 6

    A) 12
    B) 11.1
    C) 15
    D) 7
    E) 13.5

The correct answer is A:) 12. The median is the middle number when they are all arranged lowest to highest (or highest to lowest). Which in this case is 12.

5) For an experiment to be completed correctly, it must be

    A) Precise
    B) Consistent
    C) Replicable
    D) Follow specific rules
    E) All of the above

The correct answer is E:) All of the above. An experiment must be precise, consistent, replicable (meaning someone else can do the same experiment and get the same results), and follow specific rules (the scientific method).

6) The median is also

   A) The mean
   B) The 50th percentile
   C) 1-range
   D) Highly influenced by extreme values
   E) None of the above

The correct answer is B:) The 50th percentile. The median is the 50th percentile because it is the "middle" of a set of data, so half the data points are above it, and half the data points are below it. This is true of the 50th percentile.

7) Jenny misbehaved in class by talking when she was supposed to be reading. Which of the following is a fact about her behavior?

   A) She was talking
   B) She was reading
   C) She hates school
   D) She dislikes reading
   E) She dislikes reading because she needs glasses

The correct answer is A:) She was talking. A fact is something that is true and exact. It can be an event, a behavior, etc. It may be true that she needs glasses and so reading is not enjoyable, however, it was not stated in the statement above. When you draw a conclusion, it is not a fact.

8) If it is believed that the size of a violin and the thickness of its strings determine the volume it plays at, what is/are the explanatory variable(s)?

   A) Size only
   B) Thickness of strings only
   C) Volume only
   D) Size and thickness of strings
   E) Size and volume

The correct answer is D:) Size and thickness of strings. These are the variables which it is believed result in changes in volume.

9) Which of the following is true about theories?

   A) A theory is a hypothesis
   B) A theory's main purpose it to summarize
   C) A theory is an idea
   D) A theory explains observations
   E) All of the above

The correct answer is E:) All of the above. A theory is an idea that someone has. They create a hypothesis and test it to summarize and explain observations.

10) Which of the following statements is NOT true?

   A) In operant conditioning, a person associates an action with a consequence.
   B) In classical conditioning, a person establishes a link between stimulus and response.
   C) Studies have shown that operant conditioning requires extensive neural development, and therefore cannot be applied until a subject is at least twelve years of age.
   D) Operant conditioning best explains elective actions.
   E) None of the above

The correct answer is C:) Studies have shown that operant conditioning requires extensive neural development, and therefore cannot be applied until a subject is at least twelve years of age. Studies have actually shown that operant conditioning can be used to even teach infants, although the processes do become more complex the older a person gets.

11) A theory is good if it

   A) Correctly describes an observation
   B) Is expressed clearly
   C) Is used for predicting
   D) Is consistent
   E) All of the above

The correct answer is E:) All of the above. A theory is good if it correctly and clearly describes an observation for use in predicting future behavior. It is not based on assumptions and is practical. The most important part of a theory is it's usefulness for predicting future behavior.

12) Who proposed the Theory of Primary Mental Abilities?

A) Guilford
B) Sternberg
C) Thurstone
D) Gardner
E) Spearman

The correct answer is C:) Thurstone. Thurstone was the first to propose a multiple factor model which contributed to intelligence.

13) Empowering means to

A) Divide into teams
B) To create a goal
C) A synonym for synergy
D) Increasing the capacity of individuals to make choices
E) None of the above

The correct answer is D:) Increasing the capacity of individuals to make choices. By empowering students, you are giving them the power to make their own choices.

14) According to Gardner's multiple intelligences theory, a student who works better in a group and has lots of friends most likely has what type of intelligence?

A) Interpersonal
B) Bodily-kinesthetic
C) Visual-spatial
D) Intrapersonal
E) Linguistic

The correct answer is A:) Interpersonal. The interpersonal intelligence describes people who like to interact with others. They are outgoing, have many friends and prefer group activities to working alone.

15) Which of the following do you do before teaching?

   A) Assess effectiveness
   B) Make goals
   C) Implement teaching strategies
   D) Discipline
   E) All of the above

The correct answer is B:) Make goals. Step one in the teaching model is to create goals, collect materials, and determine readiness of students. Step two in the teaching model is the time you are actually teaching, when you are implementing instructional strategies.

16) Who developed the Triarchic Model of Intelligence?

   A) Spearman
   B) Thurstone
   C) Gardner
   D) Guilford
   E) Sternberg

The correct answer is E:) Sternberg. Sternberg did not believe in one specific element that could determine a person's intelligence. His model challenged the idea of the standard IQ test.

17) The third and final step of the teaching model includes

   A) Evaluate effectiveness
   B) Review if goals were met
   C) Reevaluation student readiness
   D) All of the above
   E) None of the above

The correct answer is D:) All of the above. The final step of the teaching model includes everything done after the teaching is completed. This includes evaluating the effectives of the teaching methods and activities, reviewing if the teaching goals were actually met and reevaluating if the students were in fact ready to learn this new information.

18) Which of the following describes the experiential aspect of the Triarchic Model of Intelligence?

   A) Involves verbal, mathematical and logical skills. It is the ability to understand and analyze universal concepts.
   B) It is the ability of a person to apply their ideas to real life situations.
   C) It describes the fact that the more experience a person has, the easier it is for them to learn, and the more intelligent they are.
   D) Involves creativity, the ability to deal with new or innovative situations and divergent thinking. It is the ability for a person to come up with their own ideas.
   E) None of the above

The correct answer is D:) Involves creativity, the ability to deal with new or innovative situations and divergent thinking. It is the ability of a person to come up with their own ideas. This is also called the creative aspect.

19) Which of the following is NOT a recommended teaching behavior?

   A) Handle classroom disruptions in a low key manner
   B) Rephrase questions
   C) Relate independent activities to concepts being taught
   D) Use excessive criticism
   E) Praise students

The correct answer is D:) Use excessive criticism. Sometimes it is necessary to use criticism to communicate your expectations to students. However, using more positive methods such as praise to reward work is more effective. By handling classroom disruptions in a low key manner, the teacher is able to correct any problems by working with the individual. By rephrasing questions and using clues, students give more detailed and more correct answers to questions. These are considered recommended teaching behaviors.

20) Which of the following best describes convergent thinking?

   A) Introverted and goal oriented. Convergent thinkers flourish when left to their own devices.
   B) Logical, accurate and quick. Convergent thinkers flourish in structured settings.
   C) Talkative and outgoing. Convergent thinkers flourish in interactive group settings.
   D) Creative, innovative and resourceful. Convergent thinkers flourish in open ended situations.
   E) None of the above

The correct answer is B:) Logical, accurate and quick. Convergent thinkers flourish in structured settings. Convergent thinkers work well in analytical and structured situations, such as school.

21) Lack of education is tied closely to

   A) Poverty
   B) Crime
   C) Scholarships
   D) A & B
   E) A & C

The correct answer is D:) A & B. Poverty and crime. Individuals who have less education, who may be illiterate or do not graduate from schooling have a much higher chance of being in poverty and at risk for criminal behavior.

22) Who is known for his work in finding a way to quantify creativity?

   A) Torrance
   B) Guilford
   C) Gardner
   D) Sternberg
   E) Erikson

The correct answer is A:) Torrance. He built upon Guilford's theory of divergent thinking and created a test designed to measure creative abilities on a basis of fluency, flexibility, originality and elaboration. His test is known as the Torrance Tests of Creative Thinking.

23) John's parents are highly educated and teach graduate level classes at the local university. His education aptitude is exceptionally high. His sister Jane has a learning disability and does not do well in school. John's experience in school is successful because

   A) He is naturally bright
   B) He is raised in an environment where school is considered important
   C) He studies hard
   D) All of the above
   E) None of the above

The correct answer is D:) All of the above. The concept of nature vs. nurture has been widely debated. Nature is the concept of being born with genetics that predispose you to a certain behavior (negative like alcoholism or positive such as success in school). Nurture is the concept that the environment that you are raised in impacts your future choices. Because John has both nature and nurture impacting him, he is susceptible to both.

24) Which of the following describes identity foreclosure?

   A) A person has neither commitment nor conflict.
   B) A person has conflict but no commitment.
   C) A person has commitment but no conflict.
   D) A person has both conflict and commitment.
   E) None of the above

The correct answer is C:) A person has commitment but no conflict. When foreclosure occurs a person will have no personal basis for their beliefs because they will have accepted wholesale the things that they have been told.

25) Two word utterances are considered

   A) Prespeech
   B) Holophrase
   C) Telegraphic
   D) Multiword sentences
   E) None of the above

The correct answer is C:) Telegraphic. Telegraphic speech is when children speech in two word sentences or utterances, usually by 18 months.

26) Which of the following was a theory developed by testing IQ improvement in students when teachers were led to believe that some (randomly selected) students would be smarter than others in a class?

A) Pygmalion Effect
B) Multiple Intelligences
C) Zone of Proximal Development
D) Premack Principle
E) None of the above

The correct answer is A:) Pygmalion Effect. The theory argues that higher teacher expectations directly result in increased improvement from students.

27) Who coined the term modeling?

A) Freud
B) Piaget
C) Bandura
D) Erickson
E) Kohlberg

The correct answer is C:) Bandura. Albert Bandura was a psychologist specializing in social cognitive theory.

28) An English speaking student decides to take enter a program where the class is taught core subject areas, but also learns a foreign language. This would be an example of

A) Interference Theory
B) Maintenance Bilingual Education
C) Retroactive Inhibition
D) Transitional Bilingual Education
E) None of the above

The correct answer is B:) Maintenance Bilingual Education. The maintenance approach has a focus on enrichment of the student. It focuses on maintaining the student's primary language, while teaching them a second language as well.

29) A parent who ignores a child's temper tantrum is hoping to discourage future tantrums by

   A) Positive reinforcement
   B) Negative reinforcement
   C) Modeling
   D) Extinction
   E) Classical conditioning

The correct answer is D:) Extinction. Extinction is the process of unassociating the condition with the response. A child whose temper tantrums are ignored will cease the behavior if not positively or negatively reinforced.

30) What is the mean of the following data set?

   3, 4, 5, 9, 12, 14

   A) 5
   B) 7
   C) 7.8
   D) 8.3
   E) E)   9

The correct answer is C:) 7.8.

31) According to Freud's personality theory, which of the following is present at birth?

   A) Id
   B) Ego
   C) Superego
   D) Id and ego
   E) Superego and ego

The correct answer is A:) Id. The id is the part of the personality which is selfish, indulgent and pleasure seeking.

32) What does it mean if a person is in the 99th percentile?

   A) That they answered 99 percent of the questions correctly.
   B) That 99 percent of the people did better than they did.
   C) That only 99 percent of the people answered as many questions as they did.
   D) That they did as good as or better than 99 percent of the people.
   E) None of the above

The correct answer is D:) That they did as good as or better than a 99 percent of the people. Percentiles can be used to rank points within a group of data (in this case the person's score compared to all the other people in the same group) to each other.

33) Social smile appears at how many weeks?

   A) 2
   B) 4
   C) 7
   D) 9
   E) 13

The correct answer is C:) 7. The social smile appears at seven weeks.

34) According to Vygotsky's theory of social development, when does learning occur?

   A) When a child sees the interacts with others
   B) When a child internalizes the things they can't do
   C) Through observing the More Knowledgeable Other
   D) In the Zone of Proximal Development
   E) None of the above

The correct answer is D:) In the Zone of Proximal Development. The Zone of Proximal Development (ZPD) describes the fact that there is a gap between what the child can do with help, and what they can do on their own. When the child closes the gap, they have learned.

35) Aggression in 4 and 5 year olds is usually _____ related.

   A) People
   B) Possession
   C) Food
   D) Sleep
   E) Attention

The correct answer is B:) Possession. Aggression in that age group is usually possession related.

36) If a parent grounds a child from the computer after they fail a test, which of the following best describes the type of conditioning?

   A) Positive reinforcement
   B) Negative reinforcement
   C) Positive punishment
   D) Negative punishment
   E) No conditioning is occurring

The correct answer is D:) Negative punishment. It is negative because computer privileges were taken away, and a punishment because the point is to make it less likely the child will fail a test again.

37) Initiative vs. Guilt is Erickson's developmental stage which occurs while a

   A) Infant
   B) Toddler
   C) Preschooler
   D) School-age child
   E) Adolescent

The correct answer is C:) Preschooler. Initiative vs. Guilt is the stage where children are discovering future social roles.

38) Which of the following theories supports the idea of conditioning?

   A) Interference theory
   B) Law of Effect
   C) Multiple intelligences theory
   D) Pygmalion effect
   E) Premack principle

The correct answer is B:) Law of Effect. The Law of Effect states that if a situation or action produces a positive outcome or feeling it is more likely to be repeated. If a situation or action produces a negative outcome or feeling it will become less likely to be repeated.

39) Which is the fourth stage of Maslow's Hierarchy of Needs?

   A) Self-actualization
   B) Esteem needs
   C) Belonging and love
   D) Safety
   E) Physical needs

The correct answer is B:) Esteem needs. According to Maslow, esteem needs, how you feel as a person, is the highest stage that many people will ever reach.

40) Who proposed the idea of a general intelligence factor g?

   A) Thurstone
   B) Guilford
   C) Spearman
   D) Sternberg
   E) Gardner

The correct answer is C:) Spearman. His work became the basis for later IQ testing.

41) A full glass of water is poured into a bowl and the same amount poured into an ice cube tray. This is testing a child's

   A) Observational skills
   B) Learning ability
   C) Stage
   D) Initiative
   E) Conservation

The correct answer is E:) Conservation. Conservation is when a child can tell and understand that an amount of water stays the same, no matter what shape it is poured into.

42) According to Gardner's multiple intelligences theory, a student who is good at word games, likes poetry and listening to lectures most likely has what type of intelligence?

   A) Interpersonal
   B) Bodily-kinesthetic
   C) Visual-spatial
   D) Intrapersonal
   E) Linguistic

The correct answer is E:) Linguistic. The linguistic intelligence is the ability to use words effectively. This type of person does well at speaking, reading text and word games. They like to read and listen to lectures.

43) Who created the Law of Effect?

   A) Maslow
   B) Piaget
   C) Pavlov
   D) Thorndike
   E) Skinner

The correct answer is D:) Thorndike. Edward Thorndike studied cats and mazes to test their intelligence and learning. The Law of Effect is the probability of the recurrence of a response is generally governed by its consequence or effect generally in the form of reward or punishment.

44) Which of the following describes the componential aspect of the Triarchic Model of Intelligence?

   A) Involves verbal, mathematical and logical skills. It is the ability to understand universal concepts.
   B) It is the ability of a person to apply their ideas to real life situations.
   C) The componential aspect describes the fact that there are multiple types of intelligence being tested through the model.
   D) Involves creativity, the ability to deal with new or innovative situations and divergent thinking. It is the ability for a person to come up with their own ideas.
   E) None of the above

The correct answer is A:) Involves verbal, mathematical and logical skills. It is the ability to understand universal concepts. This is also called the analytical aspect.

45) While both Skinner and Pavlov used animals to test their theories of conditioning, what differentiates their research?

   A) The rat didn't respond to stimulus
   B) The rat never pushed the lever to get food
   C) The dog never rang the bell to get food
   D) The dog didn't respond to stimulus
   E) None of the above

The correct answer is C:) The dog never rang the bell to get food. Pavlov used classical conditioning so that every time he rang a bell, his dog would salivate. He began with ringing the bell when he fed the dog and at the conclusion of the experiment the dog, because he was expecting his dinner, would salivate. In contrast, B. F. Skinner used operant conditioning on his rat. His famous "Skinner box" trained a rat through reward to push a lever and food would come out.

46) What was the visual cliff experiment designed to test?

   A) An infant's depth perception
   B) An infant's auditory capabilities
   C) An infant's visual acuity
   D) An infant's mental capabilities
   E) An infant's hand eye coordination

The correct answer is A:) An infant's depth perception. The visual cliff experiment was designed for there to appear to be a cliff by putting a sheet of glass over an area to see whether infants would still crawl over top of it.

47) Thorndike believed that _ works better in stamping out responses then pain is at stamping them out.

   A) Pleasure
   B) Behavior
   C) Response
   D) Humanism
   E) Conditioning

The correct answer is A:) Pleasure. Thorndike believed that pleasure works better in stamping out responses then pain is at stamping them out. A twist of this idea is "you catch flies with honey than vinegar."

48) Which of the following describes identity diffusion?

   A) A person has neither commitment nor conflict.
   B) A person has conflict but no commitment.
   C) A person has commitment but no conflict.
   D) A person has commitment but no conflict.
   E) None of the above

The correct answer is A:) A person has neither commitment nor conflict. This type of person will have not had to deal with great conflict in their lives, but their identity will be "diffused," vague and undefined. They just go along with their lives accepting what they are told but with no real dedication to it.

49) Kyle pulls Nicole's hair and she screams. Dad comes to find out what is going on. The scream is the

   A) Condition
   B) Reinforcement
   C) Reinforcer
   D) Performance
   E) None of the above

The correct answer is C:) Reinforcer. The scream is the reinforcer. A reinforcer is a thing or a stimulus. The reinforcement is the effect of the stimulus, Dad coming to check on things.

50) What is the Pygmalion Effect?

   A) Using operant conditioning to make less probable actions more likely to occur by using more probable actions as reinforcers.
   B) A gap between what a child can do with help, and what they can do on their own.
   C) Describes the progression of a person's personality and self concept as the progresses through a series of psychological stages.
   D) Argues that higher teacher expectations directly result in increased improvement from students.
   E) None of the above

The correct answer is D:) Argues that higher teacher expectations directly result in increased improvement from students. The Pygmalion Effect is an example of self-fulfilling prophecy. It was developed primarily by Robert Rosenthal.

51) When a child is rewarded for any activity designed to encourage her to read, the teacher is demonstrating

   A) Role models
   B) Shaping
   C) Social learning
   D) Metacognition
   E) Cognitivism

The correct answer is B:) Shaping. Shaping is an operant conditioning technique. This is how many animals are trained, one step at a time. The closer an animal gets to performing the required task, the more they are rewarded.

52) A student moves to the United States from France. They speak only French but are placed in an English speaking class to help them learn English. However, the teacher does speak French so she can give the student a quick explanation of the concepts to the student when he needs it. This would be an example of

   A) Interference Theory
   B) Maintenance Bilingual Education
   C) Retroactive Inhibition
   D) Transitional Bilingual Education
   E) None of the above

The correct answer is D:) Transitional Bilingual Education. The transitional approach has its main focus of integrating the student in to mainstream classes. Although some of the material is taught in their native language, most of it is taught in the target language.

53) A computer uses its hard drive to store information. A child uses their

   A) Knowledge base
   B) Shaping
   C) Role model
   D) Social learning
   E) Generalization

The correct answer is A:) Knowledge base. A knowledge base is a name for the child's accumulated knowledge. Cognitive strategies are used to retrieve the information. Metacognition is the name for processing the information.

54) The Premack principle always relies on which of the following?

   A) Androgyny
   B) Positive punishment
   C) Operant conditioning
   D) Intrinsic reinforcers
   E) Cross-modal perception

The correct answer is C:) Operant conditioning. Intrinsic (emotional) reinforcers are a part of operant conditioning, but the Premack principle can use extrinsic (material) reinforcers as well, so C is the best answer.

55) What type of memory is used when there is a quick impression?

   A) Sensory
   B) Short term
   C) Long term
   D) Cognitive
   E) None of the above

The correct answer is A:) Sensory. Sensory is the type of memory is used when there is a quick impression or sensation. Iconic memory is where you store visual stimuli.

56) Which of the following describes proactive inhibition?

   A) When old memory interferes with learning new things.
   B) The inability of a person to recall something they have just heard.
   C) Describes a link between a stimulus and a response.
   D) When old memory is lost due to new memory gained.
   E) None of the above

The correct answer is D:) When old memory is lost due to new memory gained. This is especially applicable in situations where the new memory and old memory are similar.

57) What type of memory is used to access information from the last 20 seconds?

   A) Sensory
   B) Short term
   C) Long term
   D) Cognitive
   E) None of the above

The correct answer is B:) Short term. Short term memory is working or active memory used to store knowledge for about 20 seconds.

58) If a teacher rewards children with treats for participating in class, what type of conditioning is occurring?

   A) Positive reinforcement
   B) Negative reinforcement
   C) Positive punishment
   D) Negative punishment
   E) No conditioning is occurring

The correct answer is A:) Positive reinforcement. It is positive because the children are being given something, and it is reinforcement because the teacher wants to make them more likely to participate again.

59) Which of the following is a teaching strategy to improve the cognitive process?

   A) Rehearsal
   B) Elaboration
   C) Repeat
   D) Organization
   E) A, B, & D

The correct answer is E:) A, B, & D. Rehearsal (repeating the information), elaboration (using images and associations), organization (chunking, summarizing). By a teacher using these skills, they are using metacognition.

60) According to Gardner's multiple intelligences theory, a student who is sensitive to sounds and rhythm most likely has what type of intelligence?

   A) Logical-mathematical
   B) Intrapersonal
   C) Musical
   D) Bodily-kinesthetic
   E) Visual-spatial

The correct answer is C:) Musical. The musical intelligence describes people who love music, but it also extends to sounds in the environment.

61) Which of the following is when a child can't remember something unpleasant?

   A) Fading
   B) Distortion
   C) Suppression
   D) Interference
   E) Poor retrieval

The correct answer is C:) Suppression. Suppression is when a child does not remember something unpleasant.

62) Which of the following correctly lists the three elements of the Triarchic Model of intelligence?

A) Intrapersonal, interpersonal and analytical
B) Analytical, creative and practical
C) Componential, intrapersonal and practical
D) Experiential, creative and logical-mathematical
E) None of the above

The correct answer is B:) Analytical, creative and practical. These steps are also called (in order) componential, experiential and contextual.

63) Which of the following is when you can't remember something because the information is not used?

A) Fading
B) Distortion
C) Suppression
D) Interference
E) Poor retrieval

The correct answer is A:) Fading. Fading occurs when something is not very important and/or is not used often.

64) Which of the following best describes divergent thinking?

A) Introverted and goal oriented. Divergent thinkers flourish when left to their own devices.
B) Logical, accurate and quick. Divergent thinkers flourish in structured settings.
C) Talkative and outgoing. Divergent thinkers flourish in interactive group settings.
D) Creative, innovative and resourceful. Divergent thinkers flourish in open ended situations.
E) None of the above

The correct answer is D:) Creative, innovative and resourceful. Divergent thinkers flourish in open ended situations. Divergent thinkers are creative and like to find multiple innovative answers to questions.

65) Which of the following is a memory aid when you create associations with something familiar to you in order to learn and remember information?

   A) Rhymes
   B) Acronyms
   C) Link system
   D) Loci system
   E) Phonetic system

The correct answer is D:) Loci system. The loci system is when you create associations with something familiar to you in order to learn and remember information.

66) Which of the following describes identity moratorium?

   A) A person has neither commitment nor conflict.
   B) A person has conflict but no commitment.
   C) A person has commitment but no conflict.
   D) A person has both conflict and commitment.
   E) None of the above

The correct answer is B:) A person has conflict but no commitment. In this stage, a person is unhappy or angry, and has no commitment to the expectations of them or their own dreams.

67) Which of the following is the most effective method of teaching?

   A) Small class size
   B) Tutoring one-on-one
   C) Group learning
   D) Private school
   E) One teacher to five student ratio

The correct answer is B:) Tutoring one-on-one. A child can learn the most when they are being worked with one-on-one.

68) Which of the following statements is correct?

   A) Shorter wait times are preferable because they help to keep the students interested.
   B) Longer wait times are not preferable because they allow the students time to think about other things.
   C) Even increasing wait time to five seconds can have a great effect on the student's ability to form a complete response.
   D) The wait time is irrelevant to how a student answers or how well they pay attention.
   E) None of the above

The correct answer is C:) Even increasing wait time to five seconds can have a great effect on the student's ability to form a complete response.

69) Which of the following is not one of the seven intelligences?

   A) Spatial
   B) Interpersonal
   C) Musical
   D) Biographical
   E) Linguistic

The correct answer is D:) Biographical. Biographical is not an intelligence. The seven types of intelligence are: logical-mathematical, linguistic, musical, spatial, bodily kinesthetic, interpersonal, and intrapersonal.

70) What is the mode of the following data set?

   1, 2, 3, 4, 5, 6, 7

   A) 4
   B) 4.5
   C) 6
   D) 7
   E) There is no mode

The correct answer is E:) There is no mode. Because all of the numbers occur the same amount of times, there is no mode in the data set.

71) Which of the following is true about IQ tests?

   A) Fair
   B) Impartial
   C) Your score can never change
   D) Impersonal
   E) None of the above

The correct answer is E:) None of the above. IQ tests are not fair or impartial. An IQ score can change over time.

72) A class a test and achieves an average of 88 percent. The standard deviation of the test scores is 4 percent. Approximately what score on the test would have a z score of 3?

   A) 76
   B) 80
   C) 88
   D) 91
   E) 100

The correct answer is E:) 100. The formula is $z=(x-\mu)/\sigma$, therefore $3=(x-88)/4$ and $x=100$. A perfect score.

73) Producing one correct solution to a problem or situation is referred to as

   A) Postulating
   B) Divergent thinking
   C) Convergent thinking
   D) Humanistic thinking
   E) None of the above

The correct answer is C:) Convergent thinking. Convergent thinking is when you product only one solution to a problem. Divergent thinking is when you produce multiple solutions.

74) According to Gardner's multiple intelligences theory, a student who is introverted and likes to teach themselves and work in quiet environments most likely has what type of intelligence?

   A) Interpersonal
   B) Bodily-kinesthetic
   C) Visual-spatial
   D) Intrapersonal
   E) Linguistic

The correct answer is D:) Intrapersonal. The intrapersonal intelligence describes people who understand their own interests, needs and goals. They tend to be shy, but are smart and intuitive.

75) When a student has extraordinary capacity for learning they are considered

   A) Disabled
   B) ADHD
   C) Gifted
   D) Mainstream
   E) Average

The correct answer is C:) Gifted. Gifted children are exceptionally smart or bright.

76) Which of the following describes the contextual aspect of the Triarchic Model of Intelligence?

   A) Involves verbal, mathematical and logical skills. It is the ability to understand universal concepts.
   B) It is the ability of a person to apply their ideas to real life situations.
   C) The contextual aspect describes a person's ability to read between the lines, and determine what words mean in terms of how they are used.
   D) Involves creativity, the ability to deal with new or innovative situations and divergent thinking. It is the ability for a person to come up with their own ideas.
   E) None of the above

The correct answer is B:) It is the ability of a person to apply their ideas to real life situations. This is also called the practical aspect.

77) The process of mixing disabled students with average and gifted students is called

   A) Independent study
   B) Differentiating
   C) Suppression
   D) Mainstreaming
   E) Convergent

The correct answer is D:) Mainstreaming. The process of mainstreaming is to mix together all student types in order to foster normal behavior for the disadvantaged group.

78) Your mother tells you the phone number of the store that you want to call, and you are able to immediately repeat it back to her. However, just 30 seconds later when you try to make the call you can no longer remember it. Which type of memory explains this?

   A) Iconic memory
   B) Procedural memory
   C) Episodic memory
   D) Echoic memory
   E) Semantic memory

The correct answer is D:) Echoic memory. Echoic memories have to do with auditory recall. It is the recall of something that a person has just heard, and is typically stored for only three to five seconds.

79) Which of the following is NOT physiological need?

   A) Sleep
   B) Food
   C) Water
   D) Shelter
   E) Television

The correct answer is E:) Television. All of the above except television are physiological needs and are the base of Maslow's Hierarchy of Needs.

80) Which of the following is NOT true of the Individuals with Disabilities Education Act?

A) It is a federal law
B) It applies to student's age of preschool to 21.
C) It has the ultimate goal of preparing disabled students for continued education and independent living.
D) It is commonly abbreviated IDEA.
E) All of the above are true.

The correct answer is E:) All of the above are true. All of the answers correctly describe the law.

81) Which of the following is an example of an internal motivator?

A) Parent
B) Teacher
C) Guardian
D) Sibling
E) Conscience

The correct answer is E:) Conscience. An internal motivator is something that comes from within. Any other influencers that are outside of the person are considered external motivators or influencers.

82) What is the range of the following data set?

1, 2, 13, 15, 56, 25, 24

A) 19.5
B) 15
C) 55
D) From 1 to 25
E) From 1 to 56

The correct answer is C:) 55. It is important to remember that range is always a single number. To say that the range is from 1 to 56 would be like saying that 7 is from 13 to 20. It just doesn't make sense. The range is 56 (the highest number) – 1 (the lowest number).

83) Which of the following gives rewards for behaving?

   A) Premack Principle
   B) Icon Model
   C) Hierarchy of Needs
   D) Nonautocratic order
   E) Shaping

The correct answer is A:) Premack Principle. The Premack Principle gives rewards to good behavior. Another systematic reinforcement program would include a token system (ex. Classroom dollars).

84) According to Gardner's multiple intelligences theory, a student who excels in calculation based fields and likes reasoning and patterns most likely has what type of intelligence?

   A) Logical-mathematical
   B) Intrapersonal
   C) Musical
   D) Bodily-kinesthetic
   E) Visual-spatial

The correct answer is A:) Logical-mathematical. The logical-mathematical intelligence describes people who like calculating and reasoning. They may like puzzles, patterns and abstract concepts.

85) John studies two children, Kim and Stacy. He monitors their progress at ages 1, 3, 5, and 10. What type of study is this?

   A) Case study
   B) Cross sectional study
   C) Longitudinal study
   D) Survey study
   E) Twin study

The correct answer is C:) Longitudinal study. A longitudinal study is conducted over a long period of time.

86) When a person is asked, "is a mountain made of earth or water?" they know the answer due to what type of memory?

   A) Semantic memory
   B) Echoic memory
   C) Iconic memory
   D) Procedural memory
   E) Episodic memory

The correct answer is A:) Semantic memory. Semantic memory involves general conceptual knowledge that a person has which wasn't necessarily acquired at any specific point in time. This type of information is not related to specific experiences.

87) John also studied two twins who were separated at birth. He is studying the effects of nature vs. nurture. What type of study is this?

   A) Case study
   B) Cross sectional study
   C) Longitudinal study
   D) Survey study
   E) Twin study

The correct answer is E:) Twin study. A twin study is mainly used to study nature vs. nurture and heredity patterns. Most importantly, a twin study involves twins.

88) On a bell curve, the highest point represents the

   Mean
   Median
   Mode
   75th percentile

   A) I, III and IV only
   B) I and II only
   C) I, II and III only
   D) II, III, and IV only
   E) I, II, III and IV

The correct answer is C:) I, II and III only. On a bell curve, the mean and median are the same, and are the highest point (where there is the same area to the right and to the left of the point). This point is also representative of the mode. Remember that bell curves are built from histograms, so the high point is where the most data points were.

89) Fred completes a single, in-depth research project on Annabelle. This is considered a

   A) Case study
   B) Cross sectional study
   C) Longitudinal study
   D) Survey study
   E) Twin study

The correct answer is A:) Case study. A case study is a study on a single subject or person.

90) Who was the first to propose the idea of convergent and divergent thinking?

   A) Guilford
   B) Thurstone
   C) Sternberg
   D) Erikson
   E) Spearman

The correct answer is A:) Guilford. Guilford studied how different people come up with different answers to situations and proposed convergent and divergent thinking as the reason.

91) When the nation is polled on who they will vote for this is a

   A) Case study
   B) Cross sectional study
   C) Longitudinal study
   D) Survey study
   E) Twin study

The correct answer is D:) Survey study. A survey is done by random sampling to a large group of people.

91) According to Erikson, what is the first stage of development?

   A) Trust vs. Mistrust
   B) Identity Role vs. Role Confusion
   C) Generativity vs. Stagnation
   D) Initiative vs. Guilt
   E) Autonomy vs. Shame and Doubt

The correct answer is A:) Trust vs. Mistrust. This stage lasts from infancy to around 18 months.

93) Which of the following is NOT an objective test?

   A) Completion
   B) Matching
   C) True/false
   D) Essay
   E) Multiple choice

The correct answer is D:) Essay. An essay is not an objective test. Objective tests include completion, matching, true/false and multiple choice.

94) Which of the following does classical conditioning BEST explain?

   Reflexive reactions
   Unconscious actions
   Elective actions

   A) I only
   B) I and II only
   C) II and III only
   D) I, II and III
   E) I and III only

The correct answer is B:) I and II only. Classical conditioning explains reflexive and unconscious actions, but doesn't really explain elective actions, or things a person chooses to do.

95) In statistics, which of the following is the mean?

   A) The layout of the survey
   B) The index of how scores are distributed
   C) The average
   D) The % of scores that fall in a given point
   E) The z score

The correct answer is C:) The average. Mean is another word for average.

96) Which of the following describes identity achievement?

   A) A person has neither commitment nor conflict.
   B) A person has conflict but no commitment.
   C) A person has commitment but no conflict.
   D) A person has both conflict and commitment.
   E) None of the above

The correct answer is D:) A person has both conflict and commitment. This is the hoped for status. A person will have a defined believe system and decided on path. They will have developed their identity.

97) Which of the following are standard scores with a mean of 0 and a deviation of 1?

   A) Z-scores
   B) T-scores
   C) Stanine
   D) Mode
   E) None of the above

The correct answer is A:) Z-scores. A z-scores is the standard scores with a mean of 0 and a deviation of 1. A t-score is the standard scores with a mean of 50 and a deviation of 10. A Stanine test is the standard scores wtih a mean of 5 and a standard deviation of 2.

98) Which of the following is NOT one of Erikson's eight stages of development?

   A) Trust vs. Mistrust
   B) Initiative vs. Guilt
   C) Autonomy vs. Shame and Doubt
   D) Identity Role vs. Role Confusion
   E) Intimacy vs. Stagnation

The correct answer is E:) Intimacy vs. Stagnation. According to Erikson, the eight stages of development are Trust vs. Mistrust, Autonomy vs. Shame and Doubt, Initiative vs. Guilt, Industry vs. Inferiority, Identity vs. Confusion, Intimacy vs. Isolation, Generativity vs. Stagnation, and Integrity vs. Despair.

99) Find the mode of the following numbers: 5 5 8 7 9 7 1 6 4 3 2 5 5 5

   A) 5
   B) 8
   C) 7
   D) 6
   E) None of the above

The correct answer is A:) 5. The mode is the number that you have the most of. In a teaching application, the mode would be the most common score.

100) According to Gardner's multiple intelligences theory, a student who likes pictures, maps, puzzles and art most likely has what type of intelligence?

   A) Logical-mathematical
   B) Intrapersonal
   C) Musical
   D) Bodily-kinesthetic
   E) Visual-spatial

The correct answer is E:) Visual-spatial. The visual-spatial intelligence describes people who are aware of their environment and think in terms of physical space.

101) Who developed a theory of moral development that emphasized differences in the moral structures of men and women?

   A) John Watson
   B) Edwin Guthrie
   C) James Marcia
   D) Lawrence Kohlberg
   E) Carol Gilligan

The correct answer is E:) Carol Gilligan. Carol Gilligan was born in New York in 1936. She studied clinical psychology and eventually went on to teach at Harvard and work closely in research with Erik Erikson and Lawrence Kohlberg-two renowned psychological theorists. Working closely with these men, Gilligan began to feel that their moral theories were biased against women, and she developed her own theory of moral development.

102) Token economies rely on which principle to influence behavior?

   A) Identity diffusion
   B) Learned helplessness
   C) Positive reinforcement
   D) Negative reinforcement
   E) All of the above

The correct answer is C:) Positive reinforcement. Positive reinforcement is the theory that rewarding good behavior will make that behavior more likely to happen. This is the method behind token economies which are based on a pattern of rewarding good behavior with tokens.

103) Which of the following is NOT a stage of James Marcia's Identity Status Theory?

   A) Identity moratorium
   B) Identity diffusion
   C) Identity crisis
   D) Identity foreclosure
   E) Identity achievement

The correct answer is C:) Identity crisis. Marcia believed that a youth could progress through four different stages as they began developing their identity. The stages are diffusion, foreclosure, moratorium, and achievement. An individual advances through these theories as they engage in varying amounts of exploration and commitment.

104) Which of James Marcia's identity stages is characterized with high levels of commitment, and low levels of exploration?

    A) Identity diffusion
    B) Identity foreclosure
    C) Identity moratorium
    D) Identity achievement
    E) Identity stability

The correct answer is B:) Identity foreclosure. This stage occurs as a youth begins to make decisions about their future, but without questioning their values and beliefs. In other words, identity foreclosure involves a high level of commitment (being willing to make educational and work decisions) but low levels of exploration.

105) Dr. Mary Budd Rowe argued that teachers must increase their wait time

    A) From 3 seconds to 10 seconds
    B) From 1 second to 2 seconds
    C) From 5 seconds to 7 seconds
    D) From 1 second to 3-5 seconds
    E) From 1 second to 7 seconds

The correct answer is D:) From 1 second to 3-5 seconds. Rowe's studies showed that if instructors will simply increase the wait time, then it changes the whole tone of the classroom. By increasing the wait time to 3-5 seconds, students will typically give longer, better-explained, and better thought out answers.

106) Which of the following is a quality of expert teachers?

    A) Able to foster class interaction
    B) Able to integrate required curriculum with needs of individual students
    C) Able to keep the class involved, attentive and interactive
    D) Able to identify needs of specific students
    E) All of the above

The correct answer is E:) All of the above. Many different skills and abilities are involved with effective teaching. The ability to master and apply various techniques leads some teachers to be classified as experts while others remain novices.

107) What is the technical term for word recognition?

   A) Accommodation
   B) Decoding
   C) Wait time
   D) Comprehension
   E) Advance organization

The correct answer is B:) Decoding. Decoding refers to the ability to mentally group letters into recognizable groups to help increase reading speed and understanding. As students learn to better recognize familiar and recurring letter groupings as words, then they will be able to expend less effort in recognizing the word, and focus more attention on understanding what they are reading.

108) Public Law 94-142 was mean to ensure that

   A) Children with disabilities receive equal access to education
   B) Schools only hire expert teachers
   C) All students are provided with access to standardized testing
   D) Student-teacher confidentiality is maintained
   E) None of the above

The correct answer is A:) Children with disabilities receive equal access to education. Public Law 94-142, also known as the Education of All Handicapped Children Law, was the first law to ensure that children with special needs would receive an education. It was essentially the precursor to what is now the Individuals with Disabilities Education Act.

109) Which of the following disabilities is NOT covered by the Individuals with Disabilities Education Act?

   A) Traumatic brain injury
   B) Autism
   C) Orthopedic impairment
   D) Visual impairment
   E) All of the above are covered under the act

The correct answer is E:) All of the above are covered under the act. The act identifies thirteen different areas of coverage for which special education services must be provided for by the school at no cost to the parents. These are autism, deaf-blindness, deafness, emotional disturbance, hearing impairment, intellectual disability, multiple disabilities, orthopedic impairment, other health impairment (including ADHD), specific learning disabilities (dyslexia), speech or language impairment, traumatic brain injury, and visual impairment.

110) Which of the following is NOT included in an IEP?

   A) A specification of the responsibilities of the school
   B) A payment plan for the parents to fund their child's special programs
   C) Outlines of goals for the students
   D) Additional services that the school will provide
   E) All of the above are included in an IEP

The correct answer is B:) A payment plan for the parents to fund their child's special programs. The purpose of the IEP is to create a learning plan for the child with no cost to the parent.

111) The exam scores in a certain class are normally distributed. Sally learns that the z-score of her exam is 3. Which of the following is true?

   A) Sally scored a 3% on the test
   B) Sally missed only 3 questions on the test
   C) Sally scored below average on the test
   D) Sally performed in the 99th percentile on the test
   E) Both C and D

The correct answer is D:) Sally performed in the 99th percentile on the test. The z-score of a normal distribution measures the number of standard deviations a certain score is from the mean. According to the 68-95-99 rule, if Sally had a z-score of 3, or was 3 standard deviations from the mean, she must have been in the 99th percentile of the class.

112) Which psychologist based his theories about learning on habit formation?

   A) James Marcia
   B) Sigmund Freud
   C) Edwin Guthrie
   D) Carol Gillian
   E) Lawrence Kohlberg

The correct answer is C:) Edwin Guthrie. Guthrie essentially argued that a set of occurrences would elicit a response from an individual. From that point onward, that response would be associated in their mind with those occurrences, and a habit will have been formed.

113) Who is known for proposing the social development theory which states that social development precedes cognitive development?

A) Lev Vygotsky
B) Jean Piaget
C) Carol Gilligan
D) Edwin Guthrie
E) Lawrence Kohlberg

The correct answer is A:) Lev Vygotsky. Vygotsky was publishing his theories around the same time as Jean Piaget. Although the two had some similar points, Vygotsky differed in a number of ways. He believed that social development was what determined meaning. As a result, learning could be different across cultures.

114) Which of the following describes the process of accommodation?

A) A child forces all new information to fit into their current schema
B) A child begins to gradually forget all information in their currently developed schemas
C) A child must develop a new schema, or alter a current one, to understand a new situation
D) A child uses current schemas to understand a new object or situation
E) None of the above

The correct answer is C:) A child must develop a new schema, or alter a current one, to understand a new situation. Accommodation is a term that was developed by Jean Piaget. He argued that children have a different thinking process than adults because they are still developing their "schemas," or understandings of the world. Therefore the process of adaptation through assimilation and accommodation is ongoing.

115) Which of the following describes the process of assimilation?

A) A child forces all new information to fit into their current schema
B) A child begins to gradually forget all information in their currently developed schemas
C) A child must develop a new schema, or alter a current one, to understand a new situation
D) A child uses current schemas to understand a new object or situation
E) None of the above

The correct answer is D:) A child uses current schemas to understand a new object or situation. Assimilation is a term that was developed by Jean Piaget. He argued that children have a different thinking process than adults because they are still developing their "schemas," or understandings of the world. Therefore the process of adaptation through assimilation and accommodation is ongoing.

116) A z-score is a measure of

   A) Percentage difference from the average
   B) Standard deviations from the mean
   C) Median distribution of a data set
   D) How normal a set of data is
   E) Standard deviations from the median

The correct answer is B:) Standard deviations from the mean. Z-scores are a statistical measure used with normally distributed data sets. A z-score identifies the number of standard deviations a particular data point is from the mean of the curve.

117) When an individual is repeatedly subjected to an adverse stimulus over which they have no control the result is often

   A) Learned helplessness
   B) Assimilation
   C) Identity moratorium
   D) Emotional achievement
   E) None of the above

The correct answer is A:) Learned helplessness. This creates a feeling in the subject that they have no control over their situation and they stop trying to avoid the stimulus.

118) A researcher wants to determine the effect that time has on memory. Time would be the

   A) Control
   B) Dependent variable
   C) Independent variable
   D) Schema
   E) Advance organizer

The correct answer is C:) Independent variable. The independent variable is the variable that is being manipulated in an experiment. In this case, time is being studied at various quantities to determine the reaction of the dependent variable: memory.

119) Which of the following is a teaching tool used to connect old information to new information?

   A) Dependent variables
   B) Advance organizers
   C) Assimilators
   D) T scores
   E) All of the above

The correct answer is B:) Advance organizers. Advance organizers are used to create a bridge between previously studied information and new information. This helps students to feel more secure in learning the new information, to put it into context, and to recall it better later on.

120) Which of the following statements best fit with the theories of John Watson?

   A) Most personal traits are developed as a result of inheritance
   B) Women are naturally more prone to associate with ethics of care
   C) Social development is the basis for cognitive development
   D) A child's environment shapes their development
   E) None of the above

The correct answer is D:) A child's environment shapes their development. John Watson was known for the development of behaviorism. He believed that behaviors a child was exposed to would determine their future development. His work was strongly influenced by the theories of classical conditioning and the role of unconscious thought.

Test Taking Strategies

Here are some test-taking strategies that are specific to this test and to other CLEP tests in general:

- Keep your eyes on the time. Pay attention to how much time you have left.
- Read the entire question and read all the answers. Many questions are not as hard to answer as they may seem. Sometimes, a difficult sounding question really only is asking you how to read an accompanying chart. Chart and graph questions are on most CLEP tests and should be an easy free point.
- If you don't know the answer immediately, the new computer-based testing lets you mark questions and come back to them later if you have time.
- Read the wording carefully. Some words can give you hints to the right answer. There are no exceptions to an answer when there are words in the question such as always, all or none. If one of the answer choices includes most or some of the right answers, but not all, then that is not the correct answer. Here is an example:

The primary colors include all of the following:

Red, Yellow, Blue, Green
Red, Green, Yellow
Red, Orange, Yellow
Red, Yellow, Blue
None of the above

- Although item A includes all the right answers, it also includes an incorrect answer, making it incorrect. If you didn't read it carefully, were in a hurry, or didn't know the material well, you might fall for this.
- Make a guess on a question that you do not know the answer to. There is no penalty for an incorrect answer. Eliminate the answer choices that you know are incorrect. For example, this will let your guess be a 1 in 3 chance instead.

 ## *What Your Score Means*

Based on your score, you may, or may not, qualify for credit at your specific institution. At University of Phoenix, a score of 50 is passing for full credit. At Utah Valley University, the score is unpublished, the school will accept credit on a case-by-case basis. Another school, Brigham Young University (BYU) does not accept CLEP credit. To find out what score you need for credit, you need to get that information from your school's website or academic advisor.

You can score between 20 and 80 on any CLEP test. Some exams include percentile ranks. Each correct answer is worth one point. You lose no points for unanswered or incorrect questions.

 ## *Test Preparation*

How much you need to study depends on your knowledge of a subject area. If you are interested in literature, took it in school, or enjoy reading then your studying and preparation for the literature or humanities test will not need to be as intensive as someone who is new to literature.

This book is much different than the regular CLEP study guides. This book actually teaches you the information that you need to know to pass the test. If you are particularly interested in an area, or you want more information, do a quick search online. We've tried not to include too much depth in areas that are not as essential on the test. It is important to understand all major theories and concepts listed in the table of contents. It is also very important to know any bolded words.

Don't worry if you do not understand or know a lot about the area. With minimal study, you can complete and pass the test.

One of the fallacies of other test books is test questions. People assume that the **content** of the questions are similar to what will be on the test. **That is not the case.** They are only to test your "test taking skills" so for those who know to read a question carefully, there is not much added value from taking a "fake" test. However, these test questions are included to teach you additional information.

To prepare for the test, make a series of goals. Select a certain amount of time to review the information you have already studied and to learn additional material. Take notes as you study, as it will help you learn the material. The ultimate test if you are ready is to randomly choose a page out of the study guide. If you can teach it to another person without any help and answer questions, you are ready.

Legal Note

All rights reserved. This Study Guide, Book and Flashcards are protected under US Copyright Law. No part of this book or study guide or flashcards may be reproduced, distributed or stored in a retrieval system, or transmitted in any form or by any means, electronic, mechanical, photocopying, recording, or otherwise, without the prior written permission of the publisher Breely Crush Publishing, LLC. This manual is not supported by or affiliated with the College Board, creators of the CLEP test. CLEP is a registered trademark of the College Entrance Examination Board, which does not endorse this book.

FLASHCARDS

This section contains flashcards for you to use to further your understanding of the material and test yourself on important concepts, names or dates. Read the term or question then flip the page over to check the answer on the back. Keep in mind that this information may not be covered in the text of the study guide. Take your time to study the flashcards, you will need to know and understand these concepts to pass the test.

Encoding	**John Watson**
Pavlov's Dog	**Two Learning Theories**
Edward Lee Thorndike	**How many pairs of chromosomes to a cell?**
XY	**XX**

Behaviorism	How a message is stored to be recalled
Behaviorist & Cognitives	Example of Classical Conditioning
46	Law of Effect
Female	Male

Biological Approach

Behavioral Approach

Cognitive Approach

Dependent Variable

Independent Variable

Correlational Research

Erik Erickson

Most important thing to Erickson

Study and observe behavior - blank slate	Personality is linked to genetics
The variable the experiment is trying to get information about	How the mind learns and thinks
How much one variable changes in relation to each other	The variables that the experimenter controls
Development of trust	Psychoanalyst

Trust vs. Mistrust

Autonomy vs. Shame and Doubt

Initiative vs. Guilt

Industry vs. Inferiority

Identity vs. Role Confusion

Intimacy vs. Isolation

Generativity vs. Stagnation

Ego Integrity vs. Despair

Toddler	Infant
School-Age	Preschooler
Young Adult	Adolescent
Old Age	Middle-Age Adult

Jean Piaget

**Reflexive Stage
(0 - 2 months)**

Primary Circular Reactions (2 - 4 months)

**Secondary Circular Reactions
(4 - 8 months)**

**Coordination of Secondary Reactions
(8 - 12 months)**

**Tertiary Circular Reactions
(12 - 18 months)**

Invention of New Means Through Mental Combination (18 - 24 months)

**Preoperational Phase
(2 - 4 years)**

Simple reflex activity such as grasping and sucking	Cognitive theorist
Repetition of change actions to reproduce interesting consequences such as kicking one's feet to move a mobile suspended over the crib	Reflexive behaviors occur in stereotyped repetition such as opening and closing fingers repetitively
Discovery of new ways to produce the same consequence or obtain the same goal such as the infant may pull a pillow toward him in an attempt to get a toy resting on it.	Responses become coordinated into more complex sequences. Actions take on an "intentional" character
Increased use of verbal representation but speech is egocentric. The beginning of symbolic rather than simple motor play. Transductive reasoning.	Evidence of an internal representational system. Symbolizing the problemsolving sequence before actually responding. Deferred imitation.

Intuitive Phase **(4 - 7 years)**	**Period of Concrete Operation** **(7 - 11 years)**
Period of Formal Operations **(11 - 15 years)**	**Oral Stage**
Anal Stage	**Phallic Stage**
Latency Stage	**Genital Stage**

Evidence for organized, logical thought. There is the ability to perform multiple classification tasks, order objects in a logical sequence, and comprehend the principle of conservation	Speech becomes more social, less egocentric. The child has an intuitive grasp of logical concepts in some areas.
Birth - 1 year	Thought becomes more abstract, incorporating the principles of formal logic. The ability to generate abstract propositions, multiple hypotheses and their possible outcomes is evident.
3 - 6 years	1 - 3 years
Adolescence	6 - 11 years

Self-actualization	**Esteem Needs**
Belonging and Love	**Safety**
Physical Needs	**Baby Albert**
Stimulus Generalization	**Naturalistic Observation**

Level 4 need	Highest need in hierarchy - Level 5
Level 2 need	Level 3 need
Kept in a box and conditioned	Level 1 need
Search conducted by watching the subject	Something from conditioning carries over to another related area

Standard deviation	**Zone of Proximal Development**
Schemas	**Identity achievement**
Identity foreclosure	**Identity moratorium**
Identity diffusion	**Operant conditioning**

A gap between what a child can do with help, and what they can do on their own.	A description of how far away, on average, the values in a data set are from a mean.
A person has commitment but no conflict.	A mental framework through which people organize their ideas about a subject.
A person has conflict but no commitment.	A person has commitment but no conflict.
A type of conditioning in which a person associates an action with a consequence.	A person has neither commitment nor conflict.

Mean

Standard scores

Visual cliff

Pygmalion Effect

G

Classical conditioning

Interference Theory

Erikson's Theory of Psychosocial Development

Also called z scores. A measure of how many standard deviations away from the mean a value is.	Add all of the numbers in a data set and divide the total by the total number of data points.
Argues that higher teacher expectations directly result in increased improvement from students.	An experiment which created the illusion of a cliff to test what age infants develop depth perception at.
Describes a link between a stimulus and a response.	Charles Spearman's general intelligence factor which he believed could be used to quantify intelligence.
Describes the progression of a person's personality and self concept as they progress through a series of psychological stages.	Describes how learning new information has an effect on memory loss as a result of competition between information.

Divergent thinking	**Convergent thinking**
Trasitional Bilingual Education	**Maintenance Bilingual Education**
IDEA	**Scaffolding**
Advanced organizers	**Elaboration**

Emphasizes finding the one most correct answer as quickly and accurately as possible.	Emphasizes creativity and looks for new and innovative solutions to problems.
Focuses on maintaining the student's primary language, while teaching them a second language as well.	Focuses on integrating the student. Some of the material is taught in their native language, most of it is taught in the target language.
Materials used and resources provided (explicitly or inherently) when teaching.	Individuals with Disabilities Education Act. Governs how states provide education for students with disabilities.
Starting with basic principles and building up to more complex ones to create an association and aid learning.	Previously learned information which can be used to help the learner understand new information.

| Triarchic model of intelligence | Conservation |

| Metacognition | Range |

| Median | Mode |

| Episodic memory | Semantic memory |

The ability of children to recognize that changes in shape and configuration don't necessarily indicate changes in mass or fundamental property.	Sternberg's model which claimed analytical, creative and practical factors to intelligence.
The difference between the highest and lowest number in a data set.	The ability to think about thinking or control one's own thoughts.
The number which occurs most commonly in a data set.	The median is the middle number in a set of data when it is organized from lowest to highest.
The recall of general conceptual facts which are unrelated to specific experiences.	The recall of autobiographical facts, such as dates, places and emotions.

Procedural memory	Iconic memory
Echoic memory	Centration
Wait-time	Dependent variable
Independent variable	Extinction

The recall of something a person has seen for a brief period of time.	The recall of how to perform a specific, frequently performed task.
The tendency of young children to focus on one aspect of a situation.	The recall of something that a person has just heard.
The variable which changes in response to the independent variable.	The time between asking a question and calling on a student for the answer.
The weakening of a response when lack of reinforcement occurs after conditioning.	The variable which explains the change in a dependent variable.

Theory of Primary Mental Abilities

Premack principle

Shaping

Assimilation

Accommodation

Retroactive inhibition

Proactive inhibition

Z score formula

Using operant conditioning to make less probable actions more likely to occur by using more probable actions as reinforcers.

Theory argued by Thurstone which was the first to suggest multiple factors of intelligence.

When new information is encountered and can be input into the brain without changing existing ideas.

Using operant conditioning to move an existing response to a target response.

When old memory interferes with learning new things.

When new information is encountered which contradicts preexisting ideas and the brain must adapt to fit it in.

$z = (x - \mu)/\sigma$

When old memory is lost due to new memory gained.